Saints & Angels

ALSO BY DOREEN VIRTUE

Books

Mornings with the Lord

Father Therapy
(with Andrew Karpenko, M.S.W.)

The Courage to Be Creative

Don't Let Anything Dull Your Sparkle

Veggie Mama
(with Jenny Ross)

The Art of Raw Living Food
(with Jenny Ross)

Eating in the Light
(with Becky Black, M.F.T., R.D.)

Constant Craving

The Yo-Yo Diet Syndrome

Losing Your Pounds of Pain

Calendar

Angel Affirmations 2018 Calendar

Divine Guidance Card Decks

Love & Light Cards

Loving Words from Jesus

All of the above are available at your local bookstore,
or may be ordered through
Hay House USA: www.hayhouse.com®
Hay House Australia: www.hayhouse.com.au
Hay House UK: www.hayhouse.co.uk
Hay House India: www.hayhouse.co.in
Doreen's website: www.AngelTherapy.com

Saints & Angels

A Guide to Heavenly Help for
Comfort, Support, and Inspiration

DOREEN VIRTUE

HAY HOUSE, INC.

Carlsbad, California • New York City

London • Sydney • Johannesburg

Vancouver • New Delhi

Published and distributed in the United States by: Hay House, Inc.: www.hay house.com® • *Published and distributed in Australia by:* Hay House Australia Pty. Ltd.: www.hayhouse.com.au • *Published and distributed in the United Kingdom by:* Hay House UK, Ltd.: www.hayhouse.co.uk • *Distributed in Canada by:* Raincoast Books: www.raincoast.com • *Published in India by:* Hay House Publishers India: www.hayhouse.co.in

Cover and interior design: Bryn Starr Best

**Cataloging-in-Publication Data
is on file with the Library of Congress**

ISBN: 978-1-4019-5540-3

10 9 8 7 6 5 4 3 2 1
1st edition, March 2018

To Jesus of Nazareth.
Thank you for saving me!

CONTENTS

PART III: THE SAINTS

INTRODUCTION

A long time ago, my approach to spirituality was "the more friends in the spirit world, the better." I figured that as long as I stayed close to God and Jesus, I could call upon anyone in the spirit world and be protected. After all, I wasn't worshipping them, I reasoned—so I was obeying God's law.

Well, I later discovered, that's only true if you first carefully pray for God's guidance about whom to associate with and then put on "God's armor" (Ephesians 6:11). I didn't realize that it was vital to "test them to see if the spirit they have comes from God," as the Bible says (1 John 4:1–6). I had an open-door policy, and unfortunately the open door can invite in unwanted beings.

The prayers I said each day, and that I wrote and spoke about at workshops, were always addressed to the Holy Trinity. I would also call upon (not pray to, as prayers and worship only go to God) Archangel Michael and a few saints with whom I was familiar. I never felt the need to go outside of this circle, as they provided so much. Yet I didn't speak, write, or teach about the Holy Trinity as much as I wanted, for fear of offending those who didn't follow a Christian path.

That all changed while I was writing my *Loving Words from Jesus Cards* in 2015. For the first time in my life, I carefully read all of Jesus's words in the Gospels. I'd previously read parts of the Gospels, but this was the first time I read them in their entirety. My impression of Jesus had focused upon his healing and manifestation teachings such as, "Ask, and it will be given to you . . . knock, and it will be opened to you" (Matthew 7:7 ESV). The always-positive, cuddly, teddy-bear version of Jesus.

While reading the Gospels, however, I encountered Jesus's assertive side. He taught strong guidelines and boundaries that struck a chord within me. For example, Jesus said that if we're embarrassed to talk about him publicly, then he won't acknowledge us either (Matthew 10:32–33, Mark 8:38, and Luke 9:26).

Well, I had been reluctant to talk about Jesus in my writings and at workshops, because whenever I did so, some audience members would object. They'd say he was "too patriarchal," that he was a myth, that Constantine had changed the Bible, that the Bible was misogynistic, and that religions were filled with hurtful hypocrites. Wanting to avoid conflict, I left Jesus out of my teachings. This always bothered me, though, as I wanted to share my love for Jesus with others. Yet I admittedly allowed my fears about conflict to steer me in another direction.

So when I dug into Jesus's words in 2015, I realized that I needed to share openly about him—even if this risked offending some people. Needing support and seeking further biblical study, I joined and began attending a Foursquare Christian Church each Sunday. The next year, I felt guided to move to the Episcopal Church, which to me seemed like the perfect blend of biblical teachings, charitable-giving opportunities, open-mindedness, and nonjudgmentalness.

Then, in early 2017, I had a spiritual wake-up call that forever changed my life, including my spiritual beliefs and practices. I was at an Episcopal Church service, and a woman was introduced to the audience and honored for all her volunteer work. I was struck by her purity, generosity, and humbleness, and then suddenly she disappeared from view. In her place was a bigger-than-life vision of Jesus. Everyone and everything else faded away, and all I could see was Jesus standing about six feet tall, with his sacred heart clearly visible. He wore plain linen clothing, and his arms were open toward me, as if inviting me to embrace him.

He was as three-dimensional as any person, and not just a faint vision. He was a real, living, breathing person who was in front of me purposely. The light surrounding him glowed in beams as bright as the sun, as did the beams of light coming from his heart.

He didn't say a word audibly, yet I received a knowingness from his presence. First, I knew that he was real, and that Jesus knows who each of us is. I instantly knew that the stories in the Bible were true—all of it! The virgin birth, the miracles, the crucifixion, resurrection, and ascension. Stories about Jesus that I'd wrestled with—*Were they real? Myth? Distorted?*—were instantly settled for me. Jesus was and is real.

The rest of the church service was a blur. I couldn't tell you who was at church with me, or how I drove home afterward. Yet the moment I was home, I went online to research what I'd just seen. I typed "Jesus sacred heart lights" in the Internet search engine, and immediately saw paintings called "The Divine Mercy," which depicted a vision of St. Maria Faustina's. My vision of Jesus was similar, except there were golden rays of light shining completely around his heart, instead of the downward-pointing red and white light rays of St. Maria's vision.

I was filled with questions by this vision. Was this Jesus healing me? Inspiring me to be more like the woman who was introduced at church that day as being a mega-volunteer? Was he calling me to follow him more closely? As I prayed about these questions, I felt guided to share my vision by creating a little YouTube video of my vision. Several months later, I worked with the artist Howard David Johnson to re-create my vision of Jesus for a painting that I adore.

Two weeks later, as I was falling asleep, I had another vision. I saw Jesus hovering above a darkened Earth, sending golden light from his heart to awaken and protect everyone on the planet. The vision seemed simultaneously metaphorical and literal, as if it represented dark energy covering the planet and also perhaps some prophetic message about a worldwide power outage. In both cases, Jesus was and is helping us all.

I began reading the Bible each morning and praying more than ever to be led as God willed. After all, I'd mostly surrendered my willfulness after it almost got me killed in an armed carjacking in 1995 when I hadn't listened to God's warning. So I was accustomed to praying for and following God's will . . . most of the time. I confess there were occasions when I didn't ask God for guidance before making choices and taking action. And those were the times when I had to run to God later to fix the mess I'd made!

It occurred to me that I'd never been baptized, as the Unity Church I attended in childhood didn't offer baptisms. I'd never even thought about being baptized before! An inner knowingness, perhaps from the Holy Spirit, guided me to rectify this. So I asked the priest at my Episcopal Church, Father David, if he'd perform the baptism, and he agreed. I attended two meetings with him to prepare for the ceremony.

This church holds their baptisms at the ocean, and on February 25, 2017, the day of my baptism, the sea was churning with strong waves and currents. I gulped, but Father David and my husband, Michael, assured me that they'd hold on to me. Wearing a long white dress, I was walked into the ocean at sunset, and Father David began the ceremony, which culminated in me being immersed three times for the Father, Son, and Holy Spirit.

I had imagined having an epiphany or a divine revelation during the baptism. Instead of having insights, though, I had a sensation of a spiritual detox. I felt myself being cleansed of attachments and lower energies.

After we walked out of the ocean, Father David drew a cross on my forehead with oil that had been prayed over by the Episcopal Bishop (an amazingly humble and learned man who officiated my confirmation a few months later). As the cross was being drawn, Father David looked me in the eyes and pronounced, "You are now sealed by the Holy Spirit, and marked as Christ's own forever." His words made me gasp, as I realized the eternal commitment just made. The permanency of this spiritual shift was unlike any other agreement into which I'd ever entered. And I took the commitment to heart.

The baptism changed everything, as promised in Scripture: "And that water is a picture of baptism, which now saves you, not by removing dirt from your body, but as a response to God from a clean conscience" (1 Peter 3:21). I've always been sensitive to energies, and I felt that strong presence of the Holy Spirit and heard his teachings. (While I realize that some people experience the Holy Spirit as a feminine energy, I sense the Holy Spirit as a male teacher.)

I continued to hungrily study the Bible, including reading it from cover to cover and attending Bible study groups. The Bible is filled with messages that are essential knowledge for our modern age, as well as comforting messages and inspiring stories. My studies moved me to create this book, a collection of stories and information to deepen your own relationship with God, the angels, and saints.

In Part I of this book, "The Holy Trinity," we'll discuss how you can connect with God through prayer, as this is an important tool you can use to grow closer to God, Jesus, and Holy Spirit. You'll also come to better understand who you are, through your connection with the Trinity. Later, in Part II, "The Angels," we'll look at what the Word of God says about angelic beings, including the amazing angel stories of the Bible, and descriptions of the roles that angels fulfill in our lives. Finally, Part III focuses on 42 saints, whose stories inspire us to follow God's guidance and live a godly life.

One of the reasons why I'm including saints in this book is because I am so inspired by their lives! Saints were courageous people during their earthly lifetimes, people who faced tremendous suffering and criticism while they stuck to their beliefs.

People often turn to saints, angels, and other deities to connect them to God. Many of these icons provide an understanding of God in a manner that prompts empathy, as some of the saints' experiences on Earth may give us inspiration and hope. There's nothing wrong with honoring their legacies with the reverence they deserve, and being inspired by the spiritual example they can provide.

Just keep in mind that the Bible states that it's unacceptable to pray to anyone other than God, Jesus, and Holy Spirit: "For there is one God and one Mediator who can reconcile God and humanity—the man Christ Jesus" (1 Timothy 2:5). No one besides Jesus can mediate on our behalf, which clearly indicates that saints and angels have no authority to intercede with our pleas to them: "Therefore he [Jesus] is able, once and forever, to save those who come to God through him. He lives forever to intercede with God on their behalf" (Hebrews 7:25).

Why would God require saints, angels, or any other deity to intervene for us when he has his own Son to do it? When we want serious answers, we go straight to the top! God hears and answers our prayers, not based on who is asking but according to his will: "And this is the confidence that we have toward him, that if we ask anything according to his will he hears us" (1 John 5:14 ESV).

While we can appreciate the history and the symbolism that many of these deities bring to our spiritual life, it's important not to fall into a situation where we are worshipping, praying to, or putting our faith in anyone other than God. The First Commandment given to us leaves no room for doubt:

> You must not have any other god but me. You must not make for yourself an idol of any kind or an image of anything in the heavens or on the earth or in the sea. You must not bow down to them or worship them, for I, the Lord your God, am a jealous God who will not tolerate your affection for any other gods. (Exodus 20:3–5)

Much of the Old Testament is the story of God trying to lead his people back to focusing upon him. The chapters of the Old Testament are filled with heartbreaking stories about people who would worship idols and fall away from God. Therefore, as you're reading *Saints & Angels*, I invite you to cherish that which is holy and brings you closer to God. Just remember that he is the only one to worship, and the one who hears our prayers.

In these pages, I share with you the wonders that God offers to us, as a reference book and as inspiration. My prayer is that this book will answer some questions for you, as my own spiritual study did for me, and be a part of your ever-deepening relationship with God.

WITH LOVE AND RESPECT,

Doreen

PART I

The Holy Trinity

CONNECTING WITH THE
HOLY TRINITY

The purpose of this section of the book is to deepen your understanding of God, Jesus, and Holy Spirit, otherwise known as the "Trinity." The Holy Trinity is best learned through experience, as you can feel their loving power and presence. And yet it's also helpful to understand this intellectually as well.

As you learn more about each *Person* of the Holy Trinity, you'll be more prepared to answer the questions you have about faith and your purpose. Yes, I've used the word *Person* purposely, as each member of the Holy Trinity is living and loving. They are all one and joined together, with intersecting purposes. Just as steam, ice, and water are all forms of H_2O, so too are the Father, Son, and Holy Spirit all forms of the Divine Creator.

There are two different viewpoints of the Holy Trinity:

- The Father, Son, and Holy Spirit are three distinct and separate beings. Jesus is the Son of God, but he is not God himself.

- The Father, Son, and Holy Spirit are all aspects of the one God. Jesus was God taking on human form when he came to Earth to be our teacher and deliverer.

The doctrine of the Holy Trinity is largely embraced and agreed upon by many Christian faiths. Still, some followers are confused about the Trinity. Or, they know about "three in one," but they just don't know how to recognize each part of God individually, as a Person. Later in Part I, we will discuss each Person, as well as the unified triune God, to develop a clearer understanding.

There are many books and teachings out there that instruct you how to "do" something. There are plenty of tips on practices such as praying, witnessing, and so on. But there's a difference between learning to "do" and simply getting to know God more personally. Experiencing God in all his glory just for the sake of growing closer to him is exactly what God desires.

God is love. You can experience more of God's love by getting to know him—whether as one or three beings.

Praying to the Trinity

Many people want to know if it's all right to pray to God, Jesus, and Holy Spirit. Do we pray to just God, or can we pray to all three? According to Scripture, prayer is to be directed toward the Triune God. This means God as Father, Son, and Holy Spirit. Because all three are essentially one, you can pray to any or all.

Ways to Pray

Prayer is talking with God, Jesus, or Holy Spirit just like you would talk to another person. Prayer is taking concentrated time to connect with God. This may be in the form of making requests, offering gratitude, or sitting in silence, listening. You may pray lying down, standing up, sitting down, while you're out and about walking, and so on. It's not so much about rules, but about your sincerity and transparency with God.

Pour out your heart to him! Tell him everything! He already knows what's in your heart, but when you share it with him, you'll sense his closeness and trust him even more.

Jesus taught his disciples to pray in Matthew 6:9–13 and Luke 11:1–4. While there are several translations of the Lord's Prayer, each with minor changes in wording, I have chosen to include the most well known, which has appeared in many prayer books:

Our Father who art in heaven,
Hallowed be thy name.
Thy kingdom come.
Thy will be done on earth, as it is in heaven.
Give us this day our daily bread.
And forgive us our trespasses,
as we forgive those who trespass against us.
And lead us not into temptation,
but deliver us from evil.

Notice how in starting the prayer, Jesus addressed his Father and worshipped him. He then asked that God's will be done and asked for daily provision and for forgiveness and offered forgiveness to those who offended him. Last, he asked for help to stay away from corruption.

Many people end their prayers with "In Jesus's name, Amen," because of the message in John 14:13–14: "You can ask for anything in my name, and I will do it, so that the Son can bring glory to the Father. Yes, ask me for anything in my name, and I will do it!"

This isn't a "magic formula," however, because God will only bring you that which aligns with his will. Prayers said in Jesus's name, according to God's will, are nevertheless very powerful. An example is praying about a situation that troubles you and asking that God's will be revealed to you, or by saying "Your will be done." This prevents us from handing God a script of how we want him to answer us, helping us to instead surrender graciously and gratefully to his will.

The Lord's Prayer is simply one example of how to pray. God desires that we go to him in prayer with the simplicity and humility of a child. If you're not sure how to pray, just talk to God like you'd talk to your best friend or a trusted mentor. He's not judging what words you use. He's not concerned about how soft or loud you are. He simply wants you to be vulnerable and go to him with a sincere heart.

I also love King David's prayerful psalms, which always begin with giving glory to God, such as Psalm 8:1, "O Lord, our Lord, your majestic name fills the earth! Your glory is higher than the heavens," and Psalm 9:1, "I will praise you, Lord, with all my heart; I will tell of all the marvelous things you have done." Praising God helps you feel closer to him.

When you're not sure how to pray, ask the Holy Spirit to help you. He is with you, and the Word says that when we don't know how to pray, he prays for us. He can also show us how to pray and reveal God's will to us. Many people get stuck, judging themselves harshly for the way they pray, or comparing themselves to others. Let that type of thinking go. Prayer is not about impressing God or other people. It's about cultivating a relationship with God, Jesus, and Spirit, speaking what you feel in your heart.

Always remember that God isn't our personal genie who grants wishes. His will is beyond the scope of our human understanding. God loves us and cares for us, and the more we trust God, the less we will fight against the help he's offering to us. I love 1 John 5:14, which says, "And we are confident that he hears us whenever we ask for anything that pleases him"—in other words, when our prayers are aligned with God's will, they are answered.

FATHER GOD

God is your creator, and you were created in God's image and likeness (Genesis 1:26–27). So God is your true spiritual parent, and you are God's offspring.

Prior to Jesus's time, God was referred to by names such as *Elohim*, *Adonai*, *YHWH*, or *Lord*. Then when Jesus arrived, he referred to God as Father more than 150 times. And in many Bible verses, Jesus called God "Abba," which is a familiar and personal way of saying "my father." Well, God *is* Jesus's Father, so this makes sense. But how about for the rest of us?

Interestingly, before Jesus's time, God was called "our Father" in the Old Testament's Isaiah 63:16 and 64:8. The phrase was generalized to mean Father of the people. Jesus also encouraged his disciples to pray the Lord's Prayer with the words "Our Father."

Now, to get a real sense of how this metaphor can give us a glimpse into a Fatherly God, we must momentarily step out of the 21st century and back into the ancient days when a patriarchal society was more common. Although this may be viewed as offensively sexist by today's standards, back then the father of a family was the head of the household. He assumed full authority over everyone and was dedicated to guiding, caring for, guarding, and supporting the family.

In return, the family looked to the father to perform these duties, giving him full respect and honor, trusting that he was fulfilling them to the best of his ability. Today the roles of father, mother, and children are less defined. Many fathers are physically or emotionally absent; or, conversely, the father may be the stay-at-home parent who nurtures the children while the mother goes out and earns the income.

Since the Bible was written in a patriarchal time, writers referred to God as Father to help people better understand just who and what God was. He was described as Father in the Old

Testament various times, as he was the Father of the nation of Israel. In Exodus 4:22, God says Israel was his "firstborn son."

However, once Jesus arrived on the scene, the use of the term increased significantly. Jesus came to show God as Father in a warmer and more personal way, knowing that men, women, and children could understand God more intimately if their relationship with him was put in familial terms. After all, they already understood the nature of a family and the roles of father, mother, and child.

Jesus modeled a beautiful, profound, and deep love and respect for his Father. He taught everyone that God was Father of all. If humanity wanted to understand God better and grow more intimate with him, all they had to do was look at Jesus and learn from him.

God is many things: Creator, Redeemer, Sustainer, Healer, and so on. While he is called by many names, "Father" is a personal term. As Father, he does the same thing that good fathers all throughout time have done for their families: He provides, cares for, corrects, guides, supports, and restores. God wants us to know who he is, so he made a way for us to do so. He's a strong and loving Father, and as such, he desires a relationship with all of his children.

I often experience God as a pilot might experience an air-traffic controller: with trust that he can see what's in front of us, behind us, and all around us. Pilots can only see a finite distance, with a limited scope, so they must trust the air-traffic controller to guide them safely. It's the same way with God. Even though our rebellious egos don't like to be told what to do, for our own safety it's best to follow God's guidance.

God is our spiritual Father. As such, he blessed the earth with important aspects of himself, Jesus, and his Holy Spirit, to make a way for everyone to have a spiritual and personal relationship with him. Through belief and acceptance of Jesus and Spirit, we can have eternal life with God in his Kingdom.

God, as a Father who desires his children to spend eternity in the Light of his Kingdom, made a way for humankind to be saved from separation or darkness. Through salvation, or the belief in God and Jesus through the Spirit, a spiritual conversion occurs. We become his children, and likewise, he becomes our Father eternally.

God Is a Loving Father

If your relationship with your birth father or stepfather wasn't loving, then you may not relate to the concept of God being our Father. Many grew up with a father who wasn't able to give them the love and acceptance they needed. Some may have had abusive or absent fathers. Sometimes people project their wounded spirits onto God, thinking that he is the same way. They just can't believe or feel that God could be a loving father, because they had a very unloving father growing up. Beautifully, though, God can help you heal that part of you that was wounded by your human father.

God is loving. God is not like earthly fathers, who are subject to corruption. He supports his children, including you. If your human father wasn't the kind of father you needed and desired, know that you have a heavenly Father who is *everything* you need and desire. This is the role that God can fulfill for you, if you are open to accepting this relationship.

God as Father sees you with unconditional love in his eyes— even when you make mistakes or wander away from him for a while. He's always there to pick you up, dust you off, and welcome you back with loving arms. Whether you've been gone a day or 20 years, God as Father is eager to escort you back home, where he knows you belong. As such, he wants you to know you're never alone.

God's Fatherly Guidance

Now we get to the uncomfortable discussion about parental discipline from God. Actually, the word *discipline* has become synonymous with *abuse*, which is not what God would ever do. So, let's instead use the words *course correction*, because that's what God does: He corrects our course if we are on a dangerous trajectory and off our path. Let's be honest: If left to our own devices, we may follow whatever looks sparkly and fun, ignoring our priorities, purpose, and responsibilities. Or we may become influenced by untrustworthy people, distracted by addictions, or blocked by our insecurities and doubts. God corrects our course.

Again, using the analogy of the air-traffic controller, God can see the safest path toward our destination. If we ignore the air-traffic controller, we are missing out on valuable and potentially lifesaving guidance. Similarly, undisciplined children can get themselves into dangerous situations. Think of any public place you've been to where unsupervised children were allowed to run around, their parents seemingly heedless of their behavior. It's dangerous for the children and upsetting for those who witness these scenes. Issues arise when children grow up thinking they get to make the rules, with no guidelines as to what's right or wrong, and no consequences for breaking rules.

A good parent will correct children when they go against the rules or guidelines. God, as a loving Father, disciplines us as his children—not in the retaliatory-punishment sort of way, but in the "I care about you, so I'm helping you correct your course" way. He gives us guidelines through the Bible, his Word. If we get off track, God may issue discipline out of love. It says in Hebrews 12:6, "the Lord disciplines those he loves," meaning that he cares enough about you to correct your path.

God wants you to know that he is your loving Father, who only desires the best for you. This is why he gives you his Word as a guide for you to navigate life. He also gave Jesus as an earthly model for you to learn from. If by chance he must discipline, he will, but it will always be with respect and kindness. For example, he may remove you from a toxic situation or take away an item that could hurt you. If you're a parent, you can certainly understand how such discipline can teach and train a youngster in ways that will ultimately benefit him or her.

God as a Fatherly Inheritance

Do you know someone who has inherited a fortune from their family? People tend to talk about the advantages conferred on those who have received an inheritance through their family line, sometimes wishing they too had riches passed down to them. Fortunately, God is honored to give his children the best kind of inheritance through Jesus Christ.

Romans 8:16–17 discusses how we have been adopted into God's family and have become heirs of God and fellow heirs with Jesus. We're all sons and daughters of God, and as such, we are loved more than we can fathom (1 John 3:1). While we may not have full access to God's inheritance now, we will one day spiritually take possession of it, which will be better than we can even dream of.

As you can see, God as first Person in the Holy Trinity is a loving Father whom we can rely on for unconditional love, guidance, discipline, and full acceptance. No matter what type of father you've grown up with, know that you have a heavenly Father who adores you more than you can imagine. He's on your side, cheering for you, and has devised a redemptive plan for you to spend eternity with him in his Kingdom. How amazing is that!

Praying to Father God

You can find many people praying to God all throughout the Bible, calling on him in times of need as well as honoring, praising, and worshipping him in prayer. When Jesus was asked by his disciples how to pray, he said, "This is how you should pray . . ." (Luke 11:1), and taught them the powerful "Our Father" prayer, which modeled important aspects of a prayer practice. Jesus, who prayed to his Father often, was telling them to pray to God the Father just as he did. This is a wonderful place for anyone to start to develop a prayerful relationship with their heavenly Father.

JESUS THE SON

Jesus is the second Person in the Trinity. He was sent to the earthly plane to bridge the path for all people to get to know God as Father personally. He came as God's Son, so that we can regain wholeness emotionally and spiritually through him, and enjoy the intimacy of God as Father. Many of the questions we have about who God is can be answered if we will look at Jesus. Just as we can get to know God as Father, we can get to know him through Jesus as Son.

Prophetically, the birth of Jesus as Son of God was foretold throughout the Old Testament. Isaiah 9:6 says, "For a child is born to us, a son is given to us. The government will rest on his shoulders. And he will be called: Wonderful Counselor, Mighty God, Everlasting Father, Prince of Peace." This prophecy, along with others in the Old Testament, pointed to Jesus coming one day as Messiah to bring redemption to humankind.

The Holy Mission of Jesus

The Old Testament is filled with stories of people who stopped listening to God's guidance, as well as the trouble they got in as a result. They engaged in all sorts of dangerous actions such as worshipping idols and partying instead of working. Many of the priests were teaching but not following God's commandments. Although God sent prophets to warn the people, they wouldn't listen and would sometimes kill the prophet.

So Jesus came to Earth to teach a new covenant, a new way of connecting with God. He courageously confronted the priests for their hypocrisy and empowered his disciples to heal through God. Jesus clarified that the most important commandments were to love God, and love others as ourselves (Matthew 22:36–40).

Galatians 4:4–5 says, "But when the right time came, God sent his Son, born of a woman, subject to the law. God sent him to buy freedom for us who were slaves to the law, so that he could adopt us as his very own children." Prior to Jesus's time on Earth, people would sacrifice animals to atone for their transgressions. Jesus allowed himself to be a living sacrifice to atone for all of humanity. God also raised Jesus from the dead for the resurrection and ascension, showing that Jesus truly is our Lord and Savior.

This was humankind's path to avoiding the bondage by the law. The Old Testament, which enumerated over 600 laws, was heavy. Imagine trying to adhere to that many laws perfectly. God sent Jesus in the flesh to fulfill the law entirely, for every person, so that each could stand righteous before God and have fellowship with him (Romans 8:3–4).

Jesus has always been and will always be Son of the Father, performing God's will forevermore as an obedient Child. This obedience and honor is marked by a great love. Jesus says in John 14:31 that he does what his Father commands him so that the world would know that he loved the Father.

Through looking at Jesus's life on Earth, we can see just how God desires us to live. Jesus came to preach and teach what his Father wanted humanity to learn and model. If you read through the Gospels, you'll be able to get a better account of the nature of Jesus and, thus, his Father. Just as the rest of the Bible is our guide for wisdom, so is the ministry of Jesus Christ of Nazareth.

It's a beautiful relationship that the Father and Son share, and this intimacy is what God desires to share with every soul. Jesus, as the second Person in the Holy Trinity, came to do the following, among other things:

- Reveal his Father to us (Matthew 11:27)
- Bring the Kingdom of Light so that those who believe in him no longer have to dwell in darkness (John 12:46)
- Seek and save those who are lost (Luke 19:10)

- Serve humanity and give his life as ransom (Mark 10:45)
- Provide an example for living (1 Peter 2:21)

As such, Jesus desires a personal relationship with you, so that he may help you hear and follow God (Philippians 2:3–8).

Praying to Jesus

Can people pray to Jesus? Absolutely. The Word of God contains various instances wherein people prayed to the Son of God. The disciple Paul said in 1 Corinthians 1:1–2 that all believers, including himself, "call on the name of our Lord Jesus Christ." In Ephesians 5:20, he also admonished believers to pray and give thanks in the name of the Lord Jesus Christ.

St. Stephen, at the time of his death, prayed to Jesus, saying, "Lord Jesus, receive my spirit" (Acts 7:59). In a vision in Acts 9:10–18, Ananias spoke with Jesus, who sent him to lay hands on Saul. Various people prayerfully asked Jesus to heal them in the New Testament, as if he were divinity.

Jesus himself said in John 14:13, "You can ask for anything in my name, and I will do it," giving believers permission and authority to pray to him. As you can see, it is clear throughout Scripture that praying to Jesus is acceptable.

In addition, Jesus can be made the object of praise and worship as well, as many saints of old have done. Numerous prayers and songs directed at Jesus have also been penned over the years. As one Person of the Trinity, Jesus certainly welcomes and receives your prayers.

HOLY SPIRIT

The third part of the Trinity is the Holy Spirit (Matthew 28:19). To those who believe in the Triune God, the Holy Spirit is not an "it"; rather, he is a Person—God in Spirit form. To those who don't believe in Triune, the Holy Spirit is not part of God but instead is the pipeline through which God and Jesus help us and communicate with us.

Some refer to the Holy Spirit as the Holy Ghost. The Greek word *pneuma* is translated as either "spirit" or "ghost," both meaning the same thing.

Matthew 1:18 and 1:20 tell us that the Virgin Mary conceived Jesus by the Holy Spirit. Later, when Jesus was baptized, the Holy Spirit descended upon him "like a dove" (Luke 3:21–22). Finally, when Jesus ascended, the Holy Spirit was sent to us, as a teacher, comforter, and encourager. He is someone to whom you can turn when you're confused, need answers, and seek guidance: "For his Spirit searches out everything and shows us God's deep secrets" (1 Corinthians 2:10). Holy Spirit teaches us everything!

And he brings gifts! Holy Spirit gives us both spiritual gifts and fruit of the Spirit.

Spiritual Gifts

Holy Spirit coaches and guides you about how to develop, polish, and best use (and how to avoid misusing) the gifts that he discerns are part of your life purpose in 1 Corinthians 12:4–11:

> There are different kinds of spiritual gifts, but the same Spirit is the source of them all. There are different kinds of service, but we serve the same Lord. God works in different ways, but it is the same God who does the work in all of us.

A spiritual gift is given to each of us so we can help each other. To one person the Spirit gives the ability to give wise advice; to another the same Spirit gives a message of special knowledge. The same Spirit gives great faith to another, and to someone else the one Spirit gives the gift of healing. He gives one person the power to perform miracles, and another the ability to prophesy. He gives someone else the ability to discern whether a message is from the Spirit of God or from another spirit. Still another person is given the ability to speak in unknown languages, while another is given the ability to interpret what is being said. It is the one and only Spirit who distributes all these gifts. He alone decides which gift each person should have.

These spiritual gifts include:

- **Wisdom:** Discerning the best solutions to problems, according to God's word and will. This gift also involves having a spiritual talent to give wise advice in a way that others can hear and understand (1 Corinthians 12:8).

- **Knowledge:** Having the gift of "knowingness" and insights into the truth of situations. This includes the gift of clarity, with the ability to shine divine light so that others can know the truth (1 Corinthians 12:8).

- **Faith:** Retaining great faith in God, no matter what the circumstances are around you. This gift also means that the person's faith is so pure that circumstances are healed and uplifted (1 Corinthians 12:9).

- **Healing:** Being a conduit for God's healing power traveling through you to help others, according to God's will. This gift is often called upon in the holy name of Jesus of Nazareth (1 Corinthians 12:9).

- **Miracles:** Similar to the gift of healing, being a vessel of God's power to miraculously transform anyone, anything, and any situation. God is the one who chooses which miracles to perform through the person, and these miracles are used to bring faith and belief in God (1 Corinthians 12:10).

- **Prophecy:** Receiving and giving messages from the one true God. This is different from being "psychic," in which messages may be received from unknown energies. Prophecy is often a foretelling of future events, sometimes so that you or others may intervene and sometimes to warn others to stop their destructive behaviors (1 Corinthians 12:10).

  Some Christian faiths teach that there are no more prophets, and that this gift is no longer given, while others encourage those who have the gift of prophecy to use it to glorify God.

- **Discernment:** The ability to accurately distinguish whether a spirit is of God or of evil. This gift also means the person can distinguish between true and false teaching, and between desires of the flesh and spiritual guidance (1 Corinthians 12:10; see also 1 John 4:6).

- **Language:** Speaking a foreign language you've never before learned so that someone else can understand you (1 Corinthians 12:10). This was demonstrated in Acts 2:4 when the apostles were filled with the Holy Spirit after Jesus's ascension, and they began speaking in foreign languages that other people understood. Some Christians say that this means "speaking in tongues," which are not earthly languages. (This last point is controversial.)

- **Interpretation:** Being able to understand a foreign language or when someone is speaking in tongues of the Holy Spirit (1 Corinthians 12:10, 14:26–28).

Other spiritual gifts are described in Paul's letters, and there are also discussions that some people may have more than one of these gifts.

Studying the great prophets of God of the Old and New Testaments, the words of Jesus, and the Book of Acts is a wonderful way to learn about the gift of prophecy. Then, ask the Holy Spirit daily for guidance about how to develop and use this spiritual gift and how to avoid misusing it.

Above all, make sure that you don't have pride in ownership of these gifts, as viewing yourself as special or above others comes from the ego, not from the Holy Spirit:

> God has given each of you a gift from his great variety of spiritual gifts. Use them well to serve one another. Do you have the gift of speaking? Then speak as though God himself were speaking through you. Do you have the gift of helping others? Do it with all the strength and energy that God supplies. Then everything you do will bring glory to God through Jesus Christ. All glory and power to him forever and ever! (1 Peter 4:10–11)

Seeds of the Fruit of the Holy Spirit

While the above-discussed spiritual gifts are given to us as God discerns, the fruit of the Holy Spirit, in contrast, has qualities (seeds) that we develop internally with God's help.

Of note is that the fruit of the Holy Spirit is a singular *fruit*, not plural *fruits*. It is one fruit with many seeds, which grow into a richer and more fulfilling life: "The Holy Spirit produces this kind of fruit in our lives: love, joy, peace, patience, kindness, goodness, faithfulness, gentleness, and self-control" (Galatians 5:22–23).

Which of these seeds of the fruit of the Holy Spirit stand out to you? Which seeds do you feel you need to work on?

I have a sign posted above my office desk, with the seeds of the Holy Spirit fruit listed. This keeps the seeds fresh and foremost in my mind. You can do the same by posting the fruit seed names on sticky notes, or buying a premade sign from a Christian retailer or an online craftsperson, such as through etsy.com.

Freewill Choices

With the fruit of the Spirit, your freewill choices determine whether or not you spiritually grow. If you allow the Holy Spirit to make necessary changes to your life (also known as *sanctification*), cleaning up areas where you've strayed from God's will, you'll manifest these qualities. You'll glow and inspire others to return to God in their actions, heart, and consciousness. But if you resist the Holy Spirit's intervention, then he won't push it on you . . . but your spiritual potential will be delayed. Many have called the Holy Spirit "a gentleman," because he is gentle, kind, and respectful of your choices.

Holy Spirit is lovingly confrontational about the areas where we've strayed away from God's loving will. This is the process called "conviction," where you'll receive an internal message that puts a spotlight on some egoic thoughts or actions—with dignity and respect, of course. You'll suddenly feel that your ego has been exposed, which is a positive way to release the ego's unconscious control.

Holy Spirit often convicts us for being dishonest, not acting with integrity, being vain, wasting valuable time, allowing ourselves to get distracted from priorities, indulging addictions, obsessing over false idols, and other toxic behaviors. In the long run, we're grateful to the Holy Spirit for telling us the truth, and we're grateful to *ourselves* for listening.

It can feel intimidating and scary to surrender to the Holy Spirit's lead while making life changes. Keep reminding yourself that the Holy Spirit is part of God's wisdom, so he *knows* what changes will bring you true happiness and fulfillment.

Scriptures about the Holy Spirit

In John 3:8, Jesus said, "The wind blows wherever it wants. Just as you can hear the wind but can't tell where it comes from or where it is going, so you can't explain how people are born of the Spirit." We may not be able to see the Holy Spirit, but we can see how he affects people and things, just like we can't see the wind, but we see and feel its effects.

Jesus taught that once he went to be with his Father, he would pour out his Spirit to all those who would receive it. He said in John 7:37–39: "Anyone who is thirsty may come to me! Anyone who believes in me may come and drink! For the Scriptures declare, 'Rivers of living water will flow from his heart.'" (When he said "living water," he was speaking of the Spirit, who would be given to everyone believing in him. But the Spirit had not yet been given, because Jesus had not yet entered into his glory.)

In Luke 24:49, Jesus told his disciples, "And now I will send the Holy Spirit, just as my Father promised." In John 16:7, he said that it was better that he left and sent his Spirit, because Jesus as a human could only be in one place at one time, but his Spirit could be everywhere, in believers, at all times.

The Gift That God Promised

In the book of Acts, Jesus tells his disciples that once he has ascended to his Father, they should wait to receive the promise of the Father, meaning the Holy Spirit, before they continue their ministry: "Do not leave Jerusalem until the Father sends you the gift he promised, as I told you before" (Acts 1:4).

So, the disciples and others stayed in Jerusalem after Jesus ascended. They were together praying and waiting for the pouring out of the Spirit. The Bible says that many disciples and people were gathered, and on the Day of Pentecost, the promise of the Father was poured out.

The account is described in Acts 2. It says that the disciples heard the sound of a rushing wind and saw visions of fire just above people's heads. They were filled with the Spirit and began speaking in new languages. When the crowds heard these common folk speaking their languages, they were astounded and came to believe that Jesus was indeed the Messiah.

What Does the Holy Spirit Do?

Just as any person has roles that they fulfill, so does the Holy Spirit. The Word of God has a lot to say about the work of the Holy Spirit. Here, we will look at some of the ways the third Person of the Trinity operates today:

- Filling, and dwelling in, believers (John 14:17)
- Guiding us into truth (John 16:13)
- Teaching (John 14:26)
- Making us holy (1 Peter 1:2)
- Giving insight or revelation when it comes to God's Word (Acts 1:16)
- Helping us glorify the Lord (John 16:14)
- Helping believers walk in the fruit of the Spirit (Galatians 5:22–23)
- Convicting the world of sin (John 16:8)
- Interceding, or praying for us (Romans 8:26)
- Giving gifts to believers for the strengthening of the Body of Christ, the church (1 Corinthians 12:13, 27–28)
- Working in our hearts (2 Corinthians 1:22)
- Empowering and strengthening us (Ephesians 3:16)
- Giving us power to witness and tell others about God's plan of salvation (Acts 1:8)

As you can see, Holy Spirit exists to benefit each believer. If you haven't received the gift of the Holy Spirit's presence in your life, turn to God and ask to receive his indwelling presence (Luke 11:13).

Begin to cultivate a special relationship with him, trusting that he is with you all the time. Walk around your house asking the Holy Spirit what to release and what to keep (especially if you're worried about any items in your home deriving from ungodly sources). Holy Spirit desires to empower you; guide you; and give you peace, insight, and gifts. He will always tell you the truth when you ask him a question. He loves you so much!

Symbols of the Holy Spirit

A white dove is a frequent symbol of the Holy Spirit, originating from the story of Jesus's baptism, when the Holy Spirit descended upon him like a dove (Mark 1:10). Sometimes the Holy Spirit is shown with an olive branch, symbolizing peace and reminiscent of the dove in the story of Noah's ark.

Other symbols of the Holy Spirit from biblical acccounts include water, wind, and fire.

Baptism by Holy Spirit

Traditional baptism involves being dunked in the water three times by a priest or pastor. The first submersion is for the Father, the second for the Son, and the third for the Holy Spirit.

After Jesus ascended, the Holy Spirit was sent to the apostles, as described in the Book of Acts, which follows the Gospels of Matthew, Mark, Luke, and John. Many of the stories in Acts are about miraculous healings and protection involving the apostles as they taught Jews and Gentiles about Jesus. One of these miracles occurred on the Pentecost and was preceded by the sound of a windstorm from heaven (Acts 2:2).

Many people read Acts 2:3, in which the fire of the Holy Spirit settled over believers, as an invitation for all of us to be baptized purely with the Holy Spirit's symbolic fire (in addition to the traditional water baptism). Paul's words in 1 Corinthians 12:13 are also referenced to uphold this belief: "We have all been baptized into one body by one Spirit, and we all share the same Spirit."

Praying to the Holy Spirit

Paul talks about our fellowship and communion with the Spirit of God in Philippians 2:1 and 2 Corinthians 13:14. Holy Spirit welcomes believers to come to him with the same reverence, love, and intimacy with which we go to God and Jesus. Jesus himself said, "But when the Father sends the Advocate as my representative—that is, the Holy Spirit—he will teach you everything and will remind you of everything I have told you" (John 14:26).

Some people note that they have a very intimate connection with Spirit and pray often to him. They don't neglect prayer to God or Jesus, but they've cultivated a close and meaningful relationship with God as Spirit. Many people ask Jesus to come and baptize them with the fire of the Holy Spirit. And others use the phrase "Come, Holy Spirit" when they pray.

TRIUNE GOD

The Trinity is a central doctrine of Christianity. It means that there are three parts to the Godhead: Father, Son, and Holy Spirit.

God the Father created everything. Jesus, who came to Earth as the Son of God, is the second Person in the Trinity. Holy Spirit, who was given to the world after Jesus returned to his Father, is the third part of the Trinity.

Many, including me, believe that the plurality of God was the reason for the plural pronouns in Genesis 1:26: "Then God said, 'Let us make human beings in our image, to be like us.'" Who is *us*? It's the Holy Trinity.

In the Triune belief system, God is three Persons—the Father, Son, and Holy Spirit. Some find this concept challenging to understand. How can one God be three different people? How can the three be coequal, all eternal beings? The Bible states that as humans, we may not be able to fully comprehend it. It's a mystery, although Scripture says that the Holy Spirit will help us understand it (1 Corinthians 2).

Think of water. God's nature is unique, just like that of water. Water doesn't stop being water when it transitions between three states: liquid, solid, and gas. It doesn't lose its essence whether it's running from the faucet, frozen in an ice tray, or rising as steam from the teapot. Just the same, God does not lose any part of himself if he's separated into three Persons. He loses no part of his inherent identity.

Genesis 1:1 says, "In the beginning God created the heavens and the earth." The original Hebrew word for *God* in this verse is *Elohim*. Now, *Elohim* is plural, so when it says "God" created the heavens and the earth, it's referring to the Trinity: God, Jesus, and Holy Spirit.

In addition, 1 John 5:7–8 says, "So we have these three witnesses—the Spirit, the water, and the blood—and all three agree." Most theologians acknowledge that this refers to the Holy Trinity.

In understanding the Triune belief better, think about who and what you are. If someone asks you *what* you are, you may say you are a human or a person. If they ask *who* are you, you may say your name. This is your essence or identity. Your uniqueness.

Here in our dimension on Earth, things are rather simple. A human is one person. But in God's dimension, things are different. Higher. Advanced. All-encompassing.

Read what novelist C. S. Lewis says about this in his theological book *Mere Christianity*:

> On the Divine level you still find personalities; but up there you find them combined in new ways which we, who do not live on that level, cannot imagine. In God's dimension, so to speak, you find a being who is three Persons while remaining one Being, just as a cube is six squares while remaining one cube. Of course we cannot fully conceive a Being like that: just as, if we were so made that we perceived only two dimensions in space we could never properly imagine a cube. But we can get a sort of faint notion of it. And when we do, we are then, for the first time in our lives, getting some positive idea, however faint, of something super-personal—something more than a person.

It is a bit mysterious, and that's the way it's supposed to be. Paul talked about this in Ephesians 3:5, writing that the mystery of God's plan, which had been previously hidden, was now made known by the revelation of the Spirit. Paul proclaims that by the insight and revelation of the Spirit, we can come to better understand God's nature and divine plan.

As mentioned earlier, the Trinity is analogous to water existing in three different states of liquid, solid, and gas. The water can change states, yet the makeup is still H_2O in all cases. In the same way, the Triune exists as God, Jesus, and Holy Spirit.

God has created Earth and has allowed this sphere to move through time and space (which themselves are measurements for humanity's sake, because outside of the earthly realm, they do not exist). Now, God, as Creator of the sphere, came into it as a human in the form of Jesus. It is through Jesus that we have come to know God in such a loving and fatherly way. Then, once Jesus left the sphere, God sent his Spirit to continue to dwell there with humanity. The Spirit dwells inside every believer and outside as well. These three Persons of God are all one, yet have different roles.

As you can see, the Holy Trinity paints a wonderful portrait of God's various characteristics and roles. Each Person of the Trinity is equally important, and each loves you, dear one. God, Jesus, and Spirit desire an intimate relationship with you, and invite you to take a leap of faith in seeking them earnestly each day. This glorifies God, and assures you of the ability to walk in his Kingdom of light and love, now and forever.

Praying to the Triune God

The Word teaches us to pray to God in Jesus's name, by the power of the Holy Spirit. At the same time, you can pray to God, Jesus, and Spirit as individuals, too, because all are included in the Trinity. It is the Holy Spirit who can really help us in our prayer lives. He can help us pray when we don't know what to say (Romans 8:26). He can also empower our prayers.

Historically, Trinitarian prayers have been used by many in the Christian tradition. In the 4th century, the Nicene Creed referred to the Spirit "who with the Father and the Son is worshipped and glorified." Essentially, this affirms for some Christian traditions the acceptance of praying to the Trinity, just as in the early Church writings, many prayers were directed to Jesus individually.

PART II

The Angels

UNDERSTANDING
THE ANGELS

The Bible is filled with beautiful stories of God's holy angels who help people by delivering messages and offering protection.

The word *angel* comes from the Greek *aggelos*, which means "a messenger of God." God sends angels to deliver messages, to protect, and to enact his will. One of the original languages of the Bible, Hebrew, referred to angels as *elohim*, with a lowercase *e*. When God is referred to, it's always with a capital *E*: *Elohim*.

Angels appear throughout the Bible, from Genesis to Revelation. Angels also appear in the Book of Enoch (which is part of the canon of only the Ethiopian Orthodox Church and the Eritrean Orthodox Tewahedo Church) and the deuterocanonical Book of Tobit (which is part of Catholic canon).

Old Testament Angel Stories

The Old Testament angel stories referred to each angel encountered as "the angel of the Lord." Sometimes these angels would speak on behalf of God, and sometimes they would speak in God's first-person voice.

Here are the major roles of angels, and the references to them in chronological order:

- **Guardianship:** In the Garden of Eden, when Adam and Eve listened to the serpent instead of to God, they were banished from the garden. God placed cherubim angels with flaming swords at the eastern entrance to the garden to guard it (Genesis 3:24).

- **Guidance:** Genesis 16 tells the story of Abraham's
  wife, Sarah (their names were Abram and Sarai at
  the time), who couldn't bear a child, so she asked
  their servant Hagar to fill in for her and conceive a
  child with Abraham. When Hagar became pregnant,
  Sarah grew jealous and acted so harshly that Hagar
  ran away. While on the road, the angel of the Lord
  appeared to Hagar and counseled her to return in
  order to fulfill her mission of giving birth to a son.
  The angel spoke to Hagar in a first-person voice of
  God, saying: "I will give you more descendants than
  you can count" (Genesis 16:10). Her son, Ishmael, is
  considered to be the patriarch of Islam.

  Some people believe that in the story in Genesis
  18, the three visitors who told Abraham and Sarah
  that they would give birth to their own son, Isaac, are
  angels. Others believe it was a direct appearance of
  the Lord in human or angel form.

- **Delivering warning messages:** Angels helped save
  Lot and his family from the destruction of Sodom
  and Gomorrah by warning him to immediately leave
  the city. An angel tried to warn Lot's daughters'
  fiancés, but they ignored the angel and were in the
  city when it was destroyed (Genesis 19:1–3, 12–26).

- **Rescuing:** After Hagar gave birth to Ishmael and
  Sarah gave birth to Isaac, the two half brothers were
  playing. Sarah didn't like how Ishmael interacted
  with Isaac, so she ordered Abraham to send Hagar
  and her son away! Hagar and Ishmael wandered
  aimlessly through the hot desert until they ran out of
  water. Finally, the young mother put her son beneath
  a bush for shade, away from her because she couldn't
  bear to watch him die of thirst. As Ishmael cried for
  water, an angel visited them and reassured Hagar that
  God had heard their cries. The angel encouraged her

to go to her son; as she did so, "God opened Hagar's eyes," and there was a water well! They drank water and thrived in the wilderness (Genesis 21:8–21).

- **Teaching:** When God tested Abraham's faith by asking him to sacrifice his son Isaac, Abraham was willing to do whatever God asked. Before the sacrifice could occur, though, the angel of the Lord spoke to Abraham and told him not to harm his son. Then the angel spoke in God's first-person voice to tell Abraham that he'd be rewarded with many descendants because of his willingness to sacrifice everything to God (Genesis 22:1–18).

- **Dream visitations:** Jacob (the son of Isaac and grandson of Abraham) had a dream about goats that led him to return home (Genesis 16:10–13), and a famous dream called "Jacob's ladder," in which he saw angels ascending and descending a ladder or stairway to heaven (Genesis 28:12).

- **Appearing as signs from God:** As Jacob and his family were traveling home, he saw angels of God. Their presence let Jacob know that it was the right location to camp (Genesis 32:1–2).

- **Theophany:** As mentioned earlier, God takes on the form of an angel when it's necessary to warn or teach us in a process called *theophany*. As Jacob continued his journey, he met an angel who was God in angelic form. Jacob and God-as-an-angel physically wrestled all night long, and during their interaction God changed Jacob's name to Israel, which in Hebrew means "God contended" or "God prevailed" (Genesis 32:24–30).

- **Way-showing:** God told Moses that he was sending an angel before him to protect and guide him and the Israelites on their journey to the promised land.

God said, "Pay close attention to him, and obey his instructions. Do not rebel against him, for he is my representative . . ." (Exodus 23:20–23; see also Exodus 32:34). Moses gave credit to God's angel in helping rescue the Israelites from Egyptian slavery (Numbers 20:16).

- **Protecting the Ark:** God instructed Moses to cover the Ark of the Covenant with golden cherubim statues (Exodus 25:17–22). He later gave the same instructions to King David for building cherubim in the temple (1 Chronicles 28:18), which his son King Solomon enacted (2 Chronicles 3:7–13).

- **Correcting:** When a pagan prophet named Balaam was riding his donkey on a mission against God's will, the angel of the Lord stood in front of him. Only Balaam's donkey saw the angel, and he balked. Balaam began hitting his donkey, until God opened the pagan man's eyes so that he saw the angel with his sword in hand. The angel rebuked Balaam for his evil ways, including beating the donkey. Then the angel sent Balaam on his way, to deliver a message from God (Numbers 22:22–35).

- **Relaying signs from God:** The angel of God asked a man named Gideon to save Israel from the Midianites. When Gideon expressed reluctance because he didn't feel qualified, the angel spoke in God's first-person voice, saying that he would be with Gideon, helping him to win. Gideon still wasn't confident, so he asked the angel to give him proof. So the angel instructed Gideon to place his food on a nearby rock. The angel touched the food, and fire consumed and burned it. This demonstration convinced Gideon (Judges 6:11–24).

- **Annunciations:** Angels frequently announce the birth of children. As mentioned previously, the three visitors, who may have been angels or may have been God or Jesus in human form, had announced the birth of Abraham and Sarah's son, Isaac, in Genesis 18. The next annunciation was that of the forthcoming birth of Samson to his parents, who had been childless. Similar to the angel of the Lord's interaction with Gideon, the angel validated his identity by bringing fire from out of nowhere to a food offering (Judges 13:2–24).

- **Providing nourishment:** When the prophet Elijah was on the run from those who were hunting him, he went to the desert and prayed for God's help. An angel was sent to Elijah, bringing the prophet some bread on hot stones and a jar of water. Then the angel of the Lord encouraged Elijah to eat, drink water, and keep going (1 Kings 19:5–8).

- **Protection:** King David frequently referred to angels in his psalms, as did other psalmists. One contains a message about guardian angels: "For he will order his angels to protect you wherever you go" (Psalm 91:11). The famous story of Daniel surviving the lions' den because an angel shut the lions' mouths is a wonderful example of God sending angels to protect us from harm (Daniel 6:13–22).

- **Delivering and interpreting prophetic visions:** Many of the prophets received their visions and insights from the angel of the Lord. In the upcoming sections about cherubim, seraphim, and the archangels Gabriel and Michael, you'll read more about the prophets and the angels.

The prophet Zechariah had his vision of horses interpreted by the angel of the Lord (Zechariah 1:9–19). An angel also showed Zechariah a vision of the high priest Jeshua being cleansed of sin (Zechariah 3:1–7). Zechariah's next vision from an angel was seeing a solid gold lamp stand and two olive trees. The angel told Zechariah that the olive trees represent "the two anointed ones who stand in the court of the Lord of all the earth" (Zechariah 4:1–14).

Next, the angel showed him a vision of women and a basket, representing Babylon (Zechariah 5:5–11). Then the angel showed Zechariah four horses of different colors, each going in a different direction to patrol the earth, representing the spirits of heaven (Zechariah 6:1–8).

New Testament Angel Stories

Biblical scholars are quick to point out an important distinction between Old and New Testament angel visitations: In the Old Testament, references to angels use the article *the*—"the" angel of the Lord—while in the New Testament, the references are to "an" angel of the Lord. Some feel that the specificity of the word *the* may indicate that the angel of the Lord was the pre-Christ, or Jesus in angel form.

Angels of the Lord are referenced in connection with several events:

- **Annunciations:** The New Testament is home to the famous Annunciation stories of Christ and John the Baptist, which we will look at in detail in the upcoming section on Archangel Gabriel.

- **Dream guidance:** An angel of the Lord appeared to Joseph in a dream to urge him to flee with Mary and baby Jesus to escape Herod's wrath (Matthew 2:13). After Herod's death, an angel of the Lord appeared in another dream of Joseph's, urging him to take his family to Israel. Joseph followed the angel's guidance (Matthew 2:19–21).

- **Heralding the resurrection:** All four Gospels offer varying accounts of angels present at the tomb after Jesus's resurrection:

  In Matthew 28:1–7, an angel of the Lord rolled the stone away from the door and told Mary Magdalene and "the other Mary" that Jesus was risen, and for them to tell the disciples that Jesus would reappear to them in Galilee.

  In Mark 15:40, the women who approached the tomb were identified as Mary Magdalene; Mary, the mother of James; and Salome, who had been present at the crucifixion. According to this account, when they reached the tomb, they saw that the stone was rolled away, and an angel told them that Jesus had risen. The angel urged the women to tell the disciples that they would see Jesus in Galilee.

  Next, in Luke 24:1–8, two angels greet "the women from Galilee" at the tomb, with the same message of Jesus being risen. In both Mark and Luke, the angel reminds the women that in Galilee, Jesus had spoken of his resurrection.

  In John 20:11–16, two angels appear to Mary Magdalene at the tomb, and then the risen Jesus himself appears to her.

The Hierarchy of Angels

Three specific types of angels were mentioned in the Bible: *seraphim*, *cherubim*, and *archangels*. In the hierarchy-of-angels systems, the belief is that, in addition to these types of angels, the apostle Paul referred to others. Pope Gregory, Pseudo-Dionysius, St. Hildegard von Bingen, and Thomas Aquinas all subscribed to this theory.

The original teachings about the hierarchy of angels were in a manuscript claimed to have been written by Dionysius, one of the original Christians mentioned in Acts 17:34. Many of the proponents of the hierarchy-of-angels theories followed the Dionysius writing, because they assumed a contemporary of Apostle Paul would have the authority to teach about angels.

Later research revealed that the manuscript was actually written hundreds of years after the real Dionysius had passed away. Thus, the writings are attributed to Pseudo-Dionysius because *pseudo* means "impostor" or "deceptive."

The belief is that there are nine types of angels, each called a realm, or choir. These nine types of angels are divided into three groups, or spheres:

1. The angels who are closest to God:

- *Seraphim*, who sing "Holy, holy, holy is the Lord of Heaven's Armies!" (Isaiah 6:3).

- *Cherubim*, who guard the tree of life (Genesis 3:24), the Ark of the Covenant, and the temple (Exodus 25:17–22; 2 Chronicles 3:7–14; Ezekiel 10:1–22, 28:14–16; and 1 Kings 6:23–28).

- *Thrones* are mentioned by Apostle Paul (Colossians 1:16) and thought by some (Pseudo-Dionysius, Pope Gregory, St. Hildegard, and Thomas Aquinas) to be a type of angel. Others consider Paul's reference to be to a literal chair that God or a king would sit upon.

2. The angels who govern the other angels:

- *Dominions* are referred to by Apostle Paul in Ephesians 1:21 (KJV), "Far above all principality, and power, and might, and dominion, and every name that is named, not only in this world, but also in that which is to come," and Colossians 1:16 (KJV), "For by him were all things created, that are in heaven, and that are in earth, visible and invisible, whether they be thrones, or dominions, or principalities, or powers: all things were created by him, and for him." (The particular wording of the King James Vesion of the Bible is important here.) In these two writings, Paul doesn't specify that a dominion is a type of angel. Pseudo-Dionysius originated this belief that dominions are a type of governing angel.

- *Virtues* present a similar situation to dominions, with the mention of *might* in Ephesians 1:21 (KJV) variously translated as "virtue" or "leader," without any specific reference to this being a type of angel. Pseudo-Dionysius extrapolated this meaning, and others followed suit.

- *Powers* is likewise a category of angel extrapolated from the word *power* that Paul wrote in Ephesians 1:21 (KJV).

3. The angels who are closest to Earth:

- *Principalities* are mentioned by Apostle Paul in Ephesians 6:12 (KJV), in his discourse about spiritual protection: "For we wrestle not against flesh and blood, but against principalities, against powers, against the rulers of the darkness of this world, against spiritual wickedness in high places." Some interpret this statement to mean that principalities are fallen angels. In the hierarchy-of-angels belief system, though, principalities are angels who are guardians to groups of people.

- *Archangels* are the angels who manage other angels, including guardian angels, according to the hierarchy-of-angels principles. As we've noted, the word *archangel* is used sparingly in the Bible, referring only to Michael in the Books of Daniel and Jude, and to Raphael in the deuterocanonical Book of Tobit.

- *Angels* are the guardians of people, with the principal reference in Psalm 91:11: "For he will order his angels to protect you wherever you go." Judaic rabbinical literature such as the Midrash offers many principles about angels.

Fallen Angels

The term *fallen angels* is an oxymoron, meaning that the two words don't make sense in conjunction with one another. An angel by definition is a messenger for God. So if an angel rebels against God and falls as a result, then it's no longer God's messenger. However, the term is useful for purposes of understanding the heavenly origin that preceded the angel's tragic fall from grace. We can all learn from fallen angels in terms of "what not to do" and how to recognize and stay far away from them.

Admittedly, I've shied away from the topic of fallen angels in my previous writings because I didn't want to acknowledge any forms of darkness. My belief was that if we remained focused upon the positive, we'd stay spiritually safe. As I've matured in my spirituality, I've come to realize how important it is to be completely aware of "who's who" in the spirit world. In fact, the fallen angels would prefer that you be unaware of their presence, believing they don't exist, so that they can conduct their business without interruption.

Awareness of the fallen angels is a key way to discern that you're only in contact with God's holy angels. After all, 2 Corinthians 11:14 says, "Even Satan disguises himself as an angel of light." You can sense a fallen angel by its hallmark signature of leaving a trail of painful experiences. Know, however, that God gave us authority to cast out fallen angels (Mark 3:15) and send them away in the name of Jesus of Nazareth.

In Genesis 6:1–4, we read about the "sons of God" (fallen angels) who rebelliously had relations and children with human women. Their offspring are called the *nephilim*, who are considered to be demons. The apocryphal Book of Enoch also discusses the nephilim in detail, yet this book is not considered to be God-breathed inspiration.

The term *principality* is often used to describe fallen angels (Ephesians 6:12 KJV); however, this term is applied to a type of holy angel, especially in the angelic hierarchy systems (Colossians 1:16 KJV). Many scholars believe that the demons mentioned over 100 times in the Bible refer to fallen angels. Others say that Jude 6 shows that the fallen angels are all securely locked and chained, so they can't be the demons running loose in the world: "And I remind you of the angels who did not stay within the limits of authority God gave them but left the place where they belonged. God has kept them securely chained in prisons of darkness, waiting for the great day of judgment."

The story behind the fall of angels can be seen in Isaiah 14:12–25, where the prophet described the fall of the ringleader of fallen angels, Lucifer, here called "shining star":

How you are fallen from heaven,
O shining star, son of the morning!
You have been thrown down to the earth,
you who destroyed the nations of the world.
For you said to yourself,
"I will ascend to heaven and set my throne above God's stars.
I will preside on the mountain of the gods
far away in the north.

I will climb to the highest heavens
and be like the Most High."
Instead, you will be brought down to the place of the dead,
down to its lowest depths.

In Revelation 12, the chief fallen angel is symbolized by a dragon fighting with Archangel Michael, who casts out the devil dragon. Revelation 12:9 identifies the dragon as the serpent of the Garden of Eden, also known as the devil or Satan, noting that he and all his angels were sent to Earth: "This great dragon—the ancient serpent called the devil, or Satan, the one deceiving the whole world—was thrown down to the earth with all his angels."

Jesus and the Holy Spirit protect us from fallen angels, provided that we don't invite these beings into our lives, whether accidentally or consciously. We have freewill choices about who we collaborate with. Fortunately, James 2:19 says that demons (fallen angels) "tremble in terror" before God. So put your whole focus upon God (including the Holy Spirit and Jesus), and God will decide which angels to send to you. In this way, you stay spiritually safe.

Praise Belongs to God

Scripture makes it clear that praise and worship belongs to God, and not angels. We are warned not to worship angels in Revelation 19:10 and 22:8–9 and to only worship God, who created the angels. We are also not to pray to angels, but we may pray to God to send us an angel. The line of communication is that God sends us angels, not the other way around.

Angels are to be respected and regarded with reverence, but not to be specifically worshipped or prayed to. In the Bible, angels are mentioned in the context of giving comfort and protection; as part of God's plan, they are worthy of honor. However, our prayers and supplications should always be directed to God and not to any other deity, including angels. When we give thanks for our blessings, we praise God, not an angel who might have been part of a prayer that was answered.

In Acts 12:1–11, we read how King Herod Agrippa had the apostle Peter arrested and put into prison with four squads of soldiers to guard him, intending to kill him after the Passover. The night before his trial, Peter was sleeping between two soldiers, bound with chains, while guards in front of the door kept watch. Then an angel of the Lord appeared and woke Peter up, and the chains fell from his hands. The angel directed Peter to get dressed and follow him past the guards and out of the city. All the while, Peter thought it was a vision. When the angel disappeared, Peter marveled: "It's really true! . . . The Lord has sent his angel and saved me from Herod and from what the Jewish leaders had planned to do to me." Peter didn't give the praise to the angel who led him through his escape, but recognized that it was God who made it happen.

When the apostle John was given the revelation of the future by an angel, his immediate response was to fall down and worship the angel. However, the angel rebuked him and told him not to do so: "No, don't worship me. I am a servant of God, just like you and your brothers the prophets, as well as all who obey what is written in this book. Worship only God!" (Revelation 22:8–9).

Christianity teaches that believers should not pray to angels; instead, we are to ask God to send angels on our behalf. This is because God desires that his children give him the glory and worship rather than the angels. Yes, they are important, but ultimately, they are God's assistants. It is God who is giving them instructions. In the Bible, people don't pray to angels or call upon them. The only exception, which I mentioned, is the example of John the Beloved falling to his knees and praying to an angel, who stops him and insists that he not pray to or worship him, but give all glory to God.

Does this mean that we aren't to acknowledge angels in our lives? Yes, we can acknowledge them. We can acknowledge them as messengers of God and protectors. We can honor their roles as God's servants in the heavens and in the earthly realm. We can become familiar with the angels and get to know them. Even if we don't recognize them being active in our lives, we should be receptive to their unseen presence. It's one more confirmation that God is constantly aware of our needs and provides his angels to minister to us.

The Purpose of Archangels and Angels

Angels and archangels exist to help bridge heaven and Earth, operating according to God's divine plan for people, as well as for the planet.

The Bible makes it clear that God uses angels as his messengers, protectors, warriors, and friends to those in need. Most of the time, they do not make themselves known, but they are always working on God's assignments for humanity and the earth. If you wonder whether God hears and answers your prayers, rest assured that he not only hears but also gets his angels involved on your behalf.

Psalm 34:7 says, "For the angel of the Lord is a guard; he surrounds and defends all who fear him." In addition, Hebrews 13:2 says, "Don't forget to show hospitality to strangers, for some who have done this have entertained angels without realizing it!"

As you can see, God desires to use his army of angels to assist humankind in many ways. God loves you so much that he has a host of heavenly angels equipped to be of service to him for your sake. Whether it's to draw you closer to him, protect you from danger, lend you a helping hand, or simply accompany you on your journey, God cares enough to allow his ministering spirits to be quite influential in your life.

As you study the Old and New Testament, you'll find references to the archangels and angels multiple times. God continually dispatched angels to communicate his messages to his people, including Abraham, Moses, Jacob, Daniel, Gideon, the Virgin Mary, Joseph, Zechariah, and more. God used angels to protect and strengthen Jesus multiple times, as in the time of Herod's persecution (Matthew 2:13–20) and while he was in the Garden of Gethsemane (Luke 22:43).

While we don't worship or pray to angels, we definitely benefit from God sending angels to our side. Next, let's dive into the topic of the specific types of angels referenced in the BIble.

SERAPHIM

Seraphim are considered to be the highest level of the angelic realm, and closest to God.

The prophet Isaiah saw the seraphim angels when he went into the temple to pray, because he—like others—was anxious about the future. The king had just died, and a time of prosperity was replaced with uncertainty.

Isaiah was given a magnificent message when he saw a vision of the train of God's robe filling the entire temple interior. Then he saw angels, each with six wings, hovering around God. These angels, called *seraphim*, sang praise to God: "Holy, holy, holy is the Lord of Heaven's Armies! The whole earth is filled with his glory!" (Isaiah 6:3). Isaiah reported that the seraphim's sighing shook the entire temple and filled it with smoke.

He also said that the seraphim's top two wings covered their faces, the middle two were used for flight, and the bottom two covered their feet. Some people believe that the word *seraphim*, plural of the word *seraph*, means "fiery ones" or "burning ones," because of their association with smoke and hot coals.

When Isaiah realized what he was seeing, he shook with fear. He protested that he wasn't pure enough to see God's angels. After all, the Law that Moses had recorded said that only ceremoniously clean people could enter into the inner temple and connect with the Holy of Holies, which contained the Ark of the Covenant. If they were not pure, they could die upon contact with the inner sanctum. So Isaiah feared for his life.

That's when a seraph flew to Isaiah with a hot coal carried from the temple altar between tongs. The angel put the hot coal on Isaiah's lips to purify him. Then God asked Isaiah to deliver his message, and Isaiah agreed (Isaiah 6:1–9).

CHERUBIM

When we think of a cherub, a pudgy baby angel similar to Cupid no doubt comes to mind. According to Alice Wood, author of the scholarly work on cherubim called *Of Wings and Wheels*, early Jewish tradition described *cherubim* (the plural of *cherub*) as having youthful human features, based on an interpretation of the roots of the word in Hebrew translating to "youth" and "-like."

The first mention of cherubim in the Bible was after Adam and Eve disobeyed God and were escorted out of the Garden of Eden. The only description of the angels referenced a fiery sword to protect the gate so that the pair couldn't reenter the Garden (Genesis 3:24). Theologians believe that the author of the Garden of Eden story may have omitted a description of what a cherub looked like, assuming that the reader knew this information. It's still difficult to imagine a cherub baby with a flaming sword guarding a gate.

Cherubim are mentioned 57 times in the King James Version of the Bible, with most of the references pertaining to sculptures guarding the Ark of the Covenant, embroidery on the Tabernacle curtains, and large statues guarding the temple entrance. There seems to be a connection between the cherubim of the Garden of Eden and those of the Ark and the temple. God was often described in Hebrew as the Lord enthroned "between the cherubim."

The first biblical description of the cherubim's characteristics was from Ezekiel 10. The prophecies of Ezekiel were concurrent with those of Jeremiah, who warned of the destruction of Jerusalem and the temple. Ezekiel's and Jeremiah's prophecies came true, and those who survived the massacre were taken in exile to Babylon.

Ezekiel's vision was of the cherubim in the temple, which was filled with the cloud of God's presence. Ezekiel described hearing the sound of the cherubim's wings moving, a sound like the voice of God, so loud that it was audible outside of the temple. All the cherubim had human hands beneath their wings. A wheel was positioned next to each cherub, and it could move in any of the four directions.

Then Ezekiel said that each of the cherubim was covered in eyes, as were the wheels next to them. The cherubim "had eyes all over their bodies, including their hands, their backs, and their wings" (Ezekiel 10:12). Each cherub had four faces: that of an ox, human, lion, and eagle.

Ezekiel saw the wheels move as the cherubim moved, and when they flew with their wings, the wheels likewise stayed with them. The prophet said that "the spirit of the living beings was in the wheels" (Ezekiel 10:17). He watched them fly to the east gate of the temple, an allusion to the cherubim at the east gate of Eden, and realized he had seen the cherubim before when he was at the Kebar River. It was then that Ezekiel had a knowingness that they were cherubim.

ARCHANGELS

The word *archangel* means "first angel" or "chief of the angels." Archangels are considered to be the managers of guardian angels, according to Thomas Aquinas, who wrote prodigiously about the hierarchy of angels.

Why Are Some Archangels Referred to as Saints?

The title "saint" may be confusing to some, as many believe that only a human can be deemed a saint. The title comes from the Latin word *sancta*, which means "holy" one. Using this title in regard to angels has long been practiced in Catholicism.

Michael, Gabriel, and Raphael have been honored as saints in the Catholic tradition from its early days. Many people did, and still do, venerate and call upon such angels for assistance. The Catholic Feast Day for the holy archangels is September 29.

Uriel is often considered to be an archangel in the systems that recognize a fourth archangel, including in the Book of Enoch. However, he is not a Catholic saint, and he doesn't appear in the canonical Bible.

Unnamed Angels in the Bible

There are other references in the Bible where the angels are not specified by name, but the consensus view holds that they are archangels.

For example:

- While standing on the banks of the Tigris River, the prophet Daniel saw a man dressed in linen clothing: "His body looked like a precious gem. His face flashed like lightning, and his eyes flamed like torches. His arms and feet shone like polished bronze, and his voice roared like a vast multitude of people" (Daniel 10:6). Many speculate that this was Archangel Gabriel. Also, in Daniel 7:16, Daniel saw another angel who interpreted an earlier vision of his, and this angel is thought to be Gabriel as well.

- In Acts 10:3–5, Cornelius had a vision and saw an angel of God, causing him to feel afraid. The angel told him that his prayers and alms had been heard by God, and gave him a message for the apostle Peter about God's salvation.

- In Matthew 4:1–11, Jesus was tempted by Satan after spending 40 days and 40 nights fasting in the wilderness. Angels then arrived and took care of him. Angels were also present at the tomb of Jesus in Matthew 28, Mark 16, Luke 24, and John 20.

Though the Bible doesn't give these angels names, one or all of them could have been archangels.

Do Archangels Have Bodies and Wings?

Some artists portray the archangels as having bodies and wings, and sometimes carrying a sword. There are biblical descriptions of seraphim and cherubim having wings, but not of archangels. No biblical evidence supports the idea that archangels have such an appearance, though they can take on human form. Daniel's visions of Gabriel did indicate that he looked like a man.

Archangels are spiritual beings who operate for the most part in the spiritual realm. This isn't to say that they don't manifest in the earthly realm at times; they can and do. There are many eye-witness reports of angels throughout history, from biblical times until today. It's still a bit of a mystery exactly how angels operate in both realms, but they have existed since God created them and will continue on for eternity.

ARCHANGEL MICHAEL

When it comes to angels, Archangel Michael is considered the leader. As "Prince of the Heavenly Host," he is above all others in rank. The Hebrew meaning for his name is "Who is like God."

Michael is powerful, but he is not all-powerful like God. In fact, we find in Jude 1:9 that he is certainly dependent upon God for power, as well as submissive. All holy angels are ranked and submit themselves to God's authority, submission here being an honor that gives power and strength, never taking it away.

Other than what we find in Scripture and other sacred texts, not much is known about Michael. He is referred to four times in the Bible and is associated with four roles:

- To combat Satan

- To protect and rescue souls from Satan's power

- To assist God's children, especially at the hour of death

- To escort souls from Earth and bring them to judgment

In the canonical Protestant Bible, the only named archangel is Michael, in the Books of Daniel, Jude, and Revelation.

While in mourning, praying and fasting for three weeks, the prophet Daniel received a message from an angel, who was most likely Gabriel. The angel explained that he had been delayed in reaching Daniel, because an evil spirit prince had blocked him. No one had helped the angel to reach Daniel except for Michael, the archangel (Daniel 10:1–13).

Daniel's soul was then disturbed by a vision he was given of a great war that would occur between nations in which he saw the forthcoming persecution of his people, the Israelites. He then saw a vision of Jesus, his face shining brightly like lightning with eyes like fire. The vision alarmed Daniel and wiped out his strength.

The angel described to Daniel an apocalyptic future time when "Michael, the archangel who stands guard over your nation, will arise. Then there will be a time of anguish greater than any since nations first came into existence. But at that time every one of your people whose name is written in the book will be rescued" (Daniel 12:1).

In the Epistle of Jude (attributed to Judas, the brother of Jesus), the author describes Archangel Michael as saying to the devil, "The Lord rebuke you!" when the devil was arguing with Michael about Moses's body (Jude 1:9). Michael did not argue with the devil, but instead rebuked him in God's name. This was Jude's way of telling us to give all matters involving evil to God for him to judge and handle. Jude was explaining about fallen angels, and how people were disobeying God, leading to an apocalyptic end time and Judgment Day.

In the Book of Revelation, the author, John the Beloved, described a war in heaven in which "Michael and his angels fought against the dragon and his angels" (Revelation 12:7). The dragon is a symbol of the devil, and this is one of the reasons Michael is often portrayed subduing a devil or dragon with his feet and sword.

In Catholicism, Archangel Michael is St. Michael, the patron saint of police officers and security guards. He is the angel whom God sends as protection against evil forces. In paintings of Archangel Michael, he is often portrayed as a muscular man with large swanlike wings. He usually wears armor and carries a sword or a shield. In some artwork, Michael holds scales of justice.

ARCHANGEL GABRIEL

Gabriel is called an *angel*, not an archangel, in the canonical Protestant Bible; he is called an archangel in the Book of Enoch. Gabriel is the only named angel to speak in the Bible. The other angels who speak are referred to with titles such as "angel of the Lord" rather than by a proper name. Michael is named, but he does not speak directly in the Bible.

The first time we meet Gabriel in the Bible is when he explains to Daniel what the prophet's visions about "the time of the end" were about. Daniel fainted as he did so, so the angel helped him to stand (Daniel 8:16–18).

Then Gabriel returned later, and explained that Archangel Michael had helped him to reach Daniel with an important message, after the devil tried to block the two of them talking. Gabriel's message in Daniel 9:21–27 was about the arrival of Jesus as the Messiah.

The next recorded visit by Gabriel was to the priest Zechariah (not to be confused with the Old Testament prophet) to announce the birth of his forthcoming son, John the Baptist. Gabriel declared that his son would be "great in the eyes of the Lord. . . . He will be filled with the Holy Spirit, even before his birth. And he will turn many Israelites to the Lord their God" (Luke 1:15–16). Archangel Gabriel elaborated that their son would prepare the people for the coming of the Lord, and cause the rebellious people to accept the wisdom of the godly.

But Zechariah didn't believe the angel, arguing that he and his wife, Elizabeth, were too old to have children. Gabriel replied, "I am Gabriel! I stand in the very presence of God. It was he who sent me to bring you this good news!" (Luke 1:19). And because Zechariah showed faithlessness by not believing the angel's message, he was struck mute and remained speechless until the child was born. Soon afterward, Elizabeth became pregnant and gave birth to their son, as the angel had promised (Luke 1:20–25).

The next annunciation was the famous story of Gabriel telling the Virgin Mary, "You will conceive and give birth to a son, and you will name him Jesus" (Luke 1:31). Gabriel foretold that her son would reign over Israel forever and his Kingdom would never end.

When Mary asked the angel how she could have a baby as a virgin, Gabriel explained that the Holy Spirit would descend upon her. Mary obediently replied that she was the Lord's servant and said, "May everything you have said about me come true." And with that, Gabriel left (Luke 1:26–38).

An angel of the Lord next went to Mary's fiancé, Joseph, who was concerned that Mary was with child. He worried whether it was right to marry her under the circumstances. Reassuring Joseph that the child was conceived by the Holy Spirit, the angel (who, even though not specifically named, many believe was Gabriel because of the similarity of the message to the one Mary received) said: "And she will have a son, and you are to name him Jesus, for he will save his people from their sins." So Joseph did as the angel of the Lord commanded and took Mary as his wife. She remained a virgin until after her son was born (Matthew 1:18–21).

Biblical scholars believe Gabriel also shows up in other parts of the Bible, although not specifically mentioned by name. Some of the additional references to an "angel of the Lord" in the New Testament could very well have been Gabriel.

According to Christian tradition, it is believed that Gabriel is the angel who appeared to Joseph and the shepherds. He may have also been the angel who "strengthened" Jesus when he was struggling in agony in the garden of Gethsemane (Luke 22:43). Furthermore, since he was a messenger angel, he may have been the angel who spoke with the apostle John in Revelation 1:1–2.

In Catholicism, Gabriel is St. Gabriel, the patron of people who work as messengers, including those in the media, teachers, and postal workers. In artwork, Gabriel is portrayed wearing a long gown, with flowing wavy hair and androgynous facial features. The symbols of this archangel in paintings include a stem of three white lily flowers to signify purity and the Holy Trinity, and a trumpet for announcements.

Paintings of Gabriel typically depict the angel holding his hands with two fingers pointed upward. This gesture is controversial, as some believe that it's a misrepresentation and demonic influence on the artists. Others point to the hand-gesture code of the ancient Greco-Romans, the so-called orator's gestures, as the origination. Historians say that the gesture of the third finger touching the thumb is symbolic of the Greek letters for Jesus, or "the name above every name."

ARCHANGEL RAPHAEL

The story of Archangel Raphael is in the Book of Tobit, which is part of Catholic canon. This book, which was written hundreds of years B.C., describes a man named Tobit who stayed loyal in his prayers to God instead of worshipping the pagan idols, as those around him (including the king) were doing. The king punishes him by stealing his money and property, and exiling him. Soon after, Tobit became blind.

His son Tobias offered to retrieve his father's money. Along the way, Tobias met a stranger who said he would guide his travels. The stranger was Archangel Raphael, in disguise as a human. God sent Rapahel to heal both Tobit and a woman named Sarah, who had been tormented by a demon that killed her husbands on their wedding night.

Raphael helped to drive out the demon in a ceremony involving fish organs, and Tobias and Sarah were married. With Raphael's help, Tobit's money was recovered. When Tobias, Sarah, and Raphael returned to Tobit's home, the angel used ground-up fish to restore Tobit's eyesight. It's a "happily ever after" story, and that's when Raphael revealed his true identity as an archangel.

Raphael might be the angel mentioned in John 5 in a story about sick people spending time at the pool at Bethesda. The reason why they would spend time there is because "an angel of the Lord came from time to time and stirred up the water. And the first person to step in after the water was stirred was healed of whatever disease he had" (John 5:1–4). Some scholars believe that this angel was Raphael because of the healing powers generally ascribed to him.

Another biblical account of an angel whom scholars believe could have been Raphael is in Genesis 18, when three angels visited Abraham and Sarah. Although the specific names of the angels were not mentioned in the book, according to the Talmud, they were Michael, Raphael, and Gabriel (Bava Metzia 86b). It is also speculated that Raphael was the angel who healed Jacob from a thigh injury in Genesis 32.

Many people honor Archangel Raphael, particularly relying on him to protect them or heal them and their families. Of course, God is the healer, but he does use angels to minister healing at his bidding. Jesus went around healing many people throughout his ministry, and sometimes the healings may have had angelic involvement, but other times it was Jesus using the authority he had in God to bring forth healing. Those in need of healing can turn to God in prayer and allow him to heal in the way he sees fit. This may include angelic help or not.

In Catholicism, Archangel Raphael is the patron saint of travelers, the blind, and matchmakers, because of his involvement in these three situations with Tobit, Tobias, and Sarah. Raphael's name means "God heals."

Paintings of Archangel Raphael portray him holding one or more fish on a fishing line, as his primary symbol. He's also shown with a walking staff, often holding the hand of a boy or young man as a traveling companion.

ARCHANGEL URIEL

As I mentioned, Uriel is considered an archangel only in the systems that recognize a fourth archangel. However, he doesn't appear in the canonical Bible. Uriel was described in the Book of Enoch and in the Second Book of Esdras. Some scholars identify Uriel as the cherub who guarded the east gate of Eden (Genesis 3:24). He is also sometimes thought to be one of the Seven Angels mentioned in the Book of Revelation.

In the Book of Enoch, Uriel's role is described as an advocate for humans, including a messenger sent to Noah to warn him of the impending flood. Perhaps because of his connection to Noah, as well as his affinity with the weather elements of thunder and lightning, Uriel is considered to be an archangel who helps us when facing floods, earthquakes, fires, hurricanes, tornadoes, and Earth changes.

Uriel is considered to be an archangel by the Episcopal Anglican church, where he is the patron of those getting confirmed into the faith. His name means "God's light," and in artwork, he is portrayed holding a ball of fire, a lantern, or the sun itself.

GUARDIAN ANGELS

When someone talks about guardian angels, I often think of the illustration of two small children crossing a rickety bridge with a large angel hovering behind them. "Angel on the Perilous Bridge," and variations of this scene, is likely one of the most common images found on a wall in children's bedrooms. This is the personification of what we conceive guardian angels would be doing—protecting their charges—and the vision of what we imagine a heavenly host would look like. The idea of a guardian angel watching over us can be a great comfort.

Angels Represent God

Does everyone have a guardian angel? It's challenging to be factual about the subject since the term *guardian angel* isn't listed anywhere in the Bible. However, the following verses from Psalm 91 are interpreted as being about guardian angels:

- **Verse 4:** "He will cover you with his feathers. He will shelter you with his wings. His faithful promises are your armor and protection."

- **Verse 10–11:** "No evil will conquer you; no plague will come near your home. For he will order his angels to protect you wherever you go."

Many people pray by reciting Psalm 91:10–11 in times when they are afraid or when they need protection. This Scripture clearly indicates that God has angels assigned to people to keep them safe.

There are references to indicate that angels are representatives of God and can provide a connection between God and humankind. For example, Matthew 18:10 indicates that children have their own angels and those angels see God: "Beware that you don't look down on any of these little ones. For I tell you that in heaven their angels are always in the presence of my heavenly Father."

Additionally, Hebrews 1:14 says concerning angels, "Therefore, angels are only servants—spirits sent to care for people who will inherit salvation." This clearly indicates that angels are sent by God to be of some type of service to people as directed by him.

Throughout Scripture we see angels being used by God to protect his people. Genesis 18 and 19 describes how angels delivered Lot from peril, and followed God's commands to bring wrath to the cities. Furthermore, in Exodus 32:34, God tells Moses that his angels would go before him—a comforting thought indeed.

Throughout the Holy Bible—from the first book, Genesis, to the last book, Revelation—you can read about God using angels to do his work in various ways in the heavens and in the earthly realm. Angels are full of God's grace, power, and majesty. Upon God's request, they do his bidding continually, helping humankind in myriad ways. God, in his infinite love and wisdom, is so gracious with his help because he desires that every person accept salvation and inherit his Kingdom. He has massive numbers of angels to help human beings so that, ultimately, they can remain with him forever.

PART III

The Saints

Drawing Inspiration from
THE SAINTS

Saints are generally thought of as people who lived a holy life devoted to God. In fact, one of Merriam-Webster's definitions of the term *saint* is "a person who is officially recognized by the Christian church as being very holy because of the way he or she lived." Sometimes a person is called a "saint" because of their kindness or generosity, which is an alternative definition according to Webster: "a person who is very good, kind, or patient." For this book, we are focusing on the first definition, a person who is officially recognized.

There are several ways in which people interact with saints:

- **Dulia:** In Catholicism, this is the process of honoring the saints. In addition, there is the traditional practice of *hyperdulia*, which is giving special honor to Mother Mary. (Both are distinct from *latria*, which is adoration and worship of God.)

- **Inspiration:** This is the method that I choose: to be *inspired* by the amazing stories of endurance, commitment, overcoming hardships, and miracles.

- **Patronage:** This is associating a saint with a particular topic. Often they are then said to be a *patron saint* of that topic.

- **Veneration:** This may involve petitioning a saint to pray for you or to intercede with your prayers, bringing them to God on your behalf.

The Bible is clear that we are to pray only to God and to worship only God. Instead of praying to the saints, some people ask for saints to intervene on their behalf—for example, "St. Teresa, please pray for me." They believe that the saints, being in heaven, are closer to God, similar to praying to God in Jesus's name. The difference, though, is that the Bible tells us to pray in Jesus's name, but there's no mention of asking saints to intercede for us. The practice has become a long-standing tradition nonetheless, which brings many people comfort.

Christians believe in life after death, and therefore it's reasonable to believe that there are godly people in heaven who might have the "ear" of God. To pray directly to one of these personages and ask them to put in a good word for us seems rational. We have no second thoughts about asking a living friend or family member to pray for us when we have a need. If we believe in the power of prayer, it seems logical to have multiple entities, both living and dead, praying for us. Perhaps you have called upon a saint or another religion's deity and received an answer, and this has led you to believe that the figure you petitioned had a direct impact on how God ultimately answered your plea.

However, we must remember that the Bible strictly forbids mediumship (talking to the dead) and also forbids worshipping idols. If you pray to saints, please be sure that your intention is sanctioned by God. You can find out by asking Holy Spirit to assist you with your prayer practice. Holy Spirit will always be honest with you, and help you to correct anything that is unbiblical.

In Catholicism, saints aren't viewed as being "dead," however. Mother Mary and the saints are seen as living in heaven, and helping us as a mediator between the Body of Christ on Earth and in heaven.

In the Catholic and Anglican churches, saints are venerated instead of worshipped. *Veneration* means "honoring," which is neither forbidden nor encouraged in the Bible. In Revelation 5:8, John describes the elders in heaven bringing God "gold bowls filled with incense, which are the prayers of God's people." Many

Catholics believe that in this passage, John the Beloved was referring to saints praying on our behalf.

Although there is some controversy whether petitioning saints is a form of worship, we can definitely find inspiration in the lives of these saints. Their stories offer us examples of courageous perseverance and a commitment to faith in God. In our prayers and conversations with God, and through the inspiring examples of saints, we can begin to summon the peace and strength we need in order to face our fears and overcome hardships.

ST. AGATHA

Have you ever felt that life has given you too much to handle? Have you been knocked down by a swelling wave of negativity and hardship? Have you ever been in a situation where impossible obstacles stood in the way of your happiness and success? While things may seem tough now, never forget the bigger picture of God's love and his plan for you! Take inspiration from the courageous example of St. Agatha.

During her brief life in the third century A.D., St. Agatha endured repeated sessions of torture and mutilation at the hands of people who challenged her faith. However, she emerged from each trial even stronger and more powerful. Her persecution only made her more secure in her beliefs.

Much of her life was spent in prison, and she was martyred around her 20th birthday in A.D. 251. At the moments when she could have felt the deepest pain and despair, she instead allowed her faith to be reinvigorated, a quality that caused her to be misunderstood and maltreated during her life. But with the benefit of hindsight, we can look to her fine example and draw great inspiration.

Despite living in an environment of widespread political corruption, St. Agatha was a woman of great character. During her life, the Roman Emperor Trajan Decius ruled. Emperor Decius was a fierce tyrant who despised Christians. He demanded that they identify themselves, denounce their God, and even sacrifice themselves in tribute.

As you can see, it was a very hard era during which to be a Christian, yet Agatha lived her faith proudly. When she was only 15, she took a vow of chastity, dedicating herself to God with a life of prayer and service. Many men in power felt threatened by this young woman's unshakable faith and purity. She had been born with every earthly advantage—beauty, wealth, and noble origin—so they were confused about why Agatha chose the service-oriented life of being a Christian over the decadent pleasures of being rich.

When Agatha rejected the sexual advances of the corrupt Roman prefect Quintianus, he spitefully put her on trial for being a Christian. While in front of a tribunal for this "crime," Agatha explained: "I am a handmaid of Christ. That is why I bear the outward appearance of a slave. Yet this is the highest nobility, to be a slave to Christ."

Attempting to bend Agatha to his whim, Quintianus tormented her and banished her to a brothel. Still, she stayed true to her Christian faith, which further enraged Quintianus. He ordered that she be imprisoned and tortured in increasingly terrible ways, including cutting off her breasts.

Quintianus sentenced Agatha to be burned at the stake, but due to an earthquake, this never occurred. Agatha was sent back to prison instead, where she was tortured once more, being rolled over jagged rocks and blazing embers. She died in prison while saying the prayer: "Lord, my Creator, you have always protected me from the cradle. You have taken me from the love of the world and given me patience to suffer. Receive my soul."

The most incredible thing about St. Agatha's treatment was not her pain. It was the fact that she sustained worse and worse treatment, yet her religious beliefs only grew stronger and stronger. She always remained steadfast in her faith and courageous in the face of discomfort.

In artwork, St. Agatha is often depicted holding her own breasts on a platter. While this image is surprising, it's the perfect reminder of how faith gives us incredible strength when we are faced with unfathomably terrible suffering. What may seem gory and unspeakable on Earth can certainly be endured when we have the true strength and guidance that faith can provide, and which Agatha demonstrated so many times while facing the challenges of her life.

Do you have the patience to endure suffering? Times may seem tough now. But St. Agatha's last prayer reminds us that when we have God on our team, temporary hardship can always be overcome by faith and divine compassion.

Because of her stoic strength and the power of her faith, St. Agatha is one of the seven women mentioned by name in the Catholic Canon of the Mass.

St. Agatha is associated with several fire- and explosion-related miracles. Her veil was removed from her tomb in Catania after her death. When someone carried it in a procession, she is credited with preventing Mt. Etna from erupting. She is said to have interceded on Malta's behalf to prevent a Turkish invasion in 1551.

St. Agatha is the patron saint for protection against fires and natural disasters. She is also the patron saint of Sicily, bellfounders, bakers, earthquakes, jewelers, martyrs, rape victims, people suffering from breast cancer, and wet nurses.

ST. ANNE

We all have a family in one form or another, whether through biology or through choice.

Whether through our relationships with the ones who raised us or the ones we are raising, we all know the unique joys and sacrifices of the parent-child relationship. Besides our parents or our children, we also have other people in our lives who offer us guidance or who benefit from our support—regardless of age, authority, or family relationship.

Sometimes, we will clash with our parents and authority figures. We might become frustrated and angry with them, or think that their actions are totally unreasonable. On the other hand, our children—or those people who look to us as figures of authority and guidance—may question our beliefs and actions at times. They may scream at us, "Why are you doing this to me?!"

Submitting to authority can be hard, yet being the authority can be hard, too. You may even experience some of the same frustrations and doubts as you live your life as a child of God!

What is the solution? Surely, we can use St. Anne as a guide for how to react in such trying situations. She showed great devotion, even as she experienced moments that tested her faith in family. She strongly desired to have a child, but when she encountered years of difficulty in becoming pregnant, she never deserted God nor renounced him. She always kept God first and remained unwavering in her belief. If we can only do the same, then all situations will be resolved with the best possible solution.

As a couple, Anne and Joachim experienced all sides of parenting. For many years, they were childless. But late in her life, Anne gave birth to Mary the Blessed Virgin, which makes her the grandmother of Jesus Christ.

The exact circumstances of how St. Anne and St. Joachim became parents can vary from text to text. We do know that Mary was Anne and Joachim's only child. Mary's parents were well-to-do and religious; they had a happy marriage and had lived a life of contentment in Nazareth, with no children.

But on a feast day when Joachim tried to present himself to offer sacrifice in the temple, he was rebuffed. A religious leader named Reuben (who was the son of Jacob and Leah, and founder of the Israelite Tribe of Reuben) told Joachim that men with no children did not deserve to be admitted to the temple.

This was a huge blow to Joachim, and he retreated to the mountains to reflect. He did not even tell Anne where he was going, and for several days, he prayed to God for guidance.

Anne was just as distressed. She did not know why her husband had disappeared, but when she found out, she too prayed to God to remove their infertility.

When God blessed Anne and Joachim with a child, Anne was so grateful that she promised the life of her child, Mary, to the service of God. Selflessly, Anne stayed true to her word, and she gave her daughter over to the service of God when Mary was only three years old.

For years, Anne and her husband wanted nothing more in the world than to have a child. Yet as soon as they received this blessing, they focused on how they could properly thank God for answering their prayers. They put their own short-term, earthly desires aside in order to work toward the long-term, divine goal of glorifying God.

Have you ever been called to make a great sacrifice? Have you ever struggled with keeping a difficult promise?

Let yourself be comforted and inspired by the courageous example of St. Anne. She pined for a child for years, and throughout she never lost her faith or optimism. Finally, when God blessed her and Joachim with a daughter, they expressed their thanks and piety by dedicating that daughter back to the service of him.

St. Anne, through her miracle of raising the mother of Jesus, teaches us the value of trusting in God. She and her husband led moral lives of religious servitude, and they remind us of the power and value of influencing children.

Sts. Anne and Joachim are watching over us in our family interactions. They are the patron saints of childless people, grandparents, mothers, and children.

St. Anne is also the patron saint of homemakers, lace makers, miners, old-clothes dealers, seamstresses, carpenters, and equestrians.

St. Anne is often depicted holding a book, standing in front of a door, or holding Mary or Jesus.

ST. ANTHONY

Have you ever struggled to be heard? Some of us dread public speaking with a great passion! If you've had to speak before a crowd, were you worried that those present wouldn't listen? Or that they wouldn't understand?

St. Anthony reminds us that moving people with words is all about sincerity. If you are seeking courage in order to give a speech or to persuade an audience, look to his example.

St. Anthony of Padua was born Fernando Martins in Lisbon, Portugal. In his 36 years of life in the 13th century, this Catholic priest and friar of the Franciscan order traveled the globe, impressing people with his oratory skills wherever he went. He was fervently devoted to helping the poor and the sick. He touched many souls through his wide knowledge of Scripture and his persuasive powers of speech.

Anthony identified his calling very early. Fernando (as he was still known at that time) entered the religious order of St. Augustine while still a teenager. At only 15 years old, he requested to be sent to the Abbey of Santa Cruz in Coimbra, then the capital of Portugal. During nearly a decade of study in Coimbra, Fernando learned Latin and Augustinian theology, and he was probably also ordained as a priest.

A huge turning point came when Fernando saw the bodies of five Franciscan martyrs that were shipped in from Morocco. These martyred monks had preached the teachings of Christ at a mosque in Seville, and upon fleeing to Morocco, they were tortured and killed. Their remains were paraded through the monastery at Coimbra.

This moment had a powerful impact on young Fernando. Moved by the sacrifice of the monks, he made a snap decision: He would move to the Franciscan order in hopes of seeking the "glorious crown of the holy martyrs." Fernando changed his name to

Anthony, and he boarded a ship for Morocco. However, he never made it there. His ship was blown off course, and he found himself in Sicily instead. Once there, he kept a low profile, opening his heart and mind to Franciscan training.

The next big turning point came in 1222, when by chance Anthony was called upon to give a short sermon before an ordination of Dominicans and Franciscans. Though their expectations were low—maybe even nonexistent—Anthony blew the group away with his simple eloquence.

What was so great about the speech? Anthony combined excellent knowledge of Scripture, a simple and universal message, and unshakable faith. All these qualities were the key to Anthony's great skills as a public speaker and an evangelist for Christ.

Although St. Anthony's persuasive power is very much linked to his ability to spread simple, universal truths to all kinds of people, he was also responsible for "flashier" displays of the divine. For example, when he traveled to Rimini, which was filled with heretics, Anthony encountered a tough crowd. As he delivered his usual passionate, moving speeches, the crowd reacted only with fidgety boredom and disinterested silence! Not to be deterred, Anthony went for a walk and prayed about what had just happened.

When Anthony arrived at the mouth of the Marecchia River, he peered down into the water and delivered his sermon to a school of fish. Suddenly, the gathering of fish grew and grew, and the fish pushed their heads through the surface of the water, as if straining to hear Anthony's speech! This incident caused quite a commotion, of course, and the formerly unmoved Rimini townspeople gave Anthony's words and message another chance. This event led to many people converting to Christianity.

Remember the great example of St. Anthony the next time you are trying to deliver a truthful message. Even if nobody is listening, do not give up. God is on your side, and your audience may come around!

St. Anthony holds the honor of being the most quickly canonized saint—it happened less than one year after his death. He is a symbol of combatting oppression, poverty, starvation, and feeling lost. He is the patron saint of lost items, lost souls, amputees, barrenness, the elderly, fishermen, harvests, mariners, shipwrecks, pregnant women, swineherds, and travelers.

St. Anthony's patronage of lost items, lost people, and lost souls is related to his far-flung travels. It's also related to an important moment in St. Anthony's life, in which someone stole his book of psalms after he gave a speech. The psalter had great sentimental value to Anthony, as it contained extensive notes that he used to teach pupils in the Franciscan order. (The book had a high monetary value as well, as printing at the time was rare and expensive.)

We've all experienced the frustration of losing an important item! It's even more stressful when there is no easily obtainable replacement. What do you do in such situations? When you've looked everywhere and found nothing—when it seems like you'll never find a lost item again—how do you react?

St. Anthony's response was prayer. He turned to God and requested that the psalm book make its way back to him—and it did! The thief was moved to return the book, and thus was established St. Anthony's intercession in the return of lost items.

St. Barbara

Do you ever feel that you are being made to suffer due to circumstances beyond your control? Have you ever had to disguise your truth from those closest to you, just to stay safe? If so, then you can take comfort and guidance from St. Barbara, a martyred virgin who lived in the 3rd century A.D.

Barbara spent much of her life in hiding and captivity, all because her pagan father did not want to accept her strong Christian faith. She lived in a time of great religious persecution and extreme intolerance toward those who declared themselves to be Christians. She was burned, bruised, and mutilated, but she never renounced her faith. She was sentenced to death, and it was her very own father who killed her.

Barbara came from a wealthy family. After her mother died, her father, Dioscorus, directed all of his time and energy toward Barbara. But unfortunately, they clashed often. Dioscorus had a very overbearing parenting style, and Barbara and her father held opposing views on religion. He was a pagan, whereas she was a strong believer in Christ. This difference in belief tainted nearly every other issue that arose between them, including marriage, schooling, and even home design.

When it became clear that Barbara would be exceptionally attractive, Dioscorus built a tower and locked his daughter away. On the surface, this was meant to be a protective move to keep her away from the eyes of curious or lustful strangers. But Dioscorus also controlled Barbara's freedom and limited her interactions with the world. For example, he allowed only pagan teachers whom he hand-selected into the tower, despite her avowed Christianity.

While Barbara was locked away in a literal sense, her example offers lessons about how to maintain your faith even when other factors restrict your freedom. As Barbara gazed out the tower windows and enjoyed the breathtaking view of the rolling meadows on her father's property, she marveled at the beauty and vastness of God's creations. She grew strong in her faith, and she took an oath of chastity.

Unfortunately, Barbara's profound love of God was not compatible with Dioscorus's beliefs. Rumors about her beauty had spread throughout Barbara's hometown, and many men flocked to Dioscorus, requesting her hand in marriage. Barbara, of course, refused all of them, while urgently requesting that her father respect her Christianity and oath of purity.

Barbara's passionate plea convinced her father that she should be able to leave the tower periodically, so she began to widen her circle and meet more Christians. One day, Barbara encountered a priest disguised as a merchant in nearby Heliopolis. He shared with her his wisdom about the mysteries of Christianity, and he baptized her.

When Dioscorus ordered a bathhouse with two windows to be built for Barbara's use, she secretly requested that a third window be added, creating a trinity of light—the perfect symbol of her bright faith. This blessed bathhouse became the site of many miracles, and the water that ran there exhibited a powerful ability to heal. Through this act, she showed that you can embrace the miracle of God's love, even when you find yourself stuck in circumstances where nobody around you understands you!

Barbara's rocky relationship with her father deteriorated rapidly. When she revealed to him that she had ordered the third window in the bathhouse as a symbol of her Christianity, he was not pleased! She told him that his idol worship was futile, and this caused him to swing his sword at her angrily. Miraculously, she escaped his violent fury due to a spontaneous opening in the tower wall.

The final months of Barbara's life were filled with unimaginable horror. She was chased, and once she was recaptured, she was again locked up by her father, handed over to the city prefect, and cruelly tortured by merciless tormentors. Yet each night, as she stood in the light even in her prison cell, her wounds were miraculously healed. After she was sentenced to death, it was her heartless father who carried out the execution.

Barbara was willing to draw her strength from God and her beliefs, despite having an unsupportive family. Throughout her short and trial-filled life, she suffered greatly at the hands of others. But she never lost her optimism, and most importantly, she never wavered in her faith.

St. Barbara is the patron saint of people who must do dangerous jobs, including artillerymen, armorers, military engineers, gunsmiths, tunnellers, miners, and all who work with cannons and explosives. When we are in danger, some believe that St. Barbara can provide us with the assurance that we will not die without first having the chance to make confession and receive extreme unction (Last Rites).

ST. BENEDICT

Temptation . . . There may be people in your life who seem to be friends but whose actions are damaging to your faith, who influence you in ways incompatible with your morals. And the most dangerous bad influences can be so hard to spot! It may not be clear that certain people are leading you away from your beliefs. Perhaps they know how to make compelling emotional appeals, while minimizing the downside. "Don't be so uptight!" they might tease you. "What's the harm? Have a little fun!"

St. Benedict of Nursia, who lived in the 5th and 6th centuries A.D., knew this kind of temptation very well. He was born around 480, with his twin sister, Scholastica (who also later became a saint). When he was in his early adolescence, Benedict went to Rome to study rhetoric with a tutor. But the version of rhetoric he was being taught had nothing to do with making a sound argument—it was all about learning how to dazzle one's opponent with flourishes, flash, and gimmicks. It was about mastering the technique of style over substance.

Have you ever been dazzled with flashiness? Perhaps you've found yourself persuaded by something or someone, only to realize that the message underneath was hollow—or even wrong? Think of those moments, and you will realize how hard it is to turn away from splashy displays!

This is exactly the revelation that St. Benedict had. When he looked around at his fellow classmates in Rome, he was deeply troubled. He saw that they were interested only in fleeting pleasures, not eternal truth. Because they had no inner moral strength or guiding principles, they were highly susceptible to vice and corruption. So Benedict removed himself from this environment and fled to the small village of Subiaco with his tutor. He withdrew so completely that he began living as a hermit, under the guidance of Romanus, another hermit.

But even as a hermit, Benedict still faced earthly temptation! The devil came to Benedict one day and made him envision a beautiful woman. But Benedict did not succumb to this; instead, he rolled himself repeatedly in a thorny bush until all desire was killed. He emerged bloody and bruised, but he said that the wounds of his flesh cured the wounds of his soul.

Because of his holy devotion to his message and practice, St. Benedict became something of a local celebrity even during his life. Monks and other members of religious orders came to see him, hoping to learn his valuable techniques.

Benedict denied the first group of monks who approached him. He told them that his instruction would be too strict for them. Nevertheless, the monks would not be discouraged, so they began a program of study under Benedict. Of course, Benedict was right in his prediction, and the monks grew so resentful of their teacher that they tried to poison his drink. But when Benedict prayed a blessing over the cup, it shattered.

Benedict's deep mental strength drew notice and praise, and he performed many miracles. Some of the most memorable ones include saving people from death (such as when he made one monk save another monk from drowning in a lake) and demonic possession (such as when he exorcised the demon from a man who could not be helped by the local bishop or the shrines of countless holy martyrs).

Benedict went on to establish an innovative system of discipleship communities, forming the basis for the monastic system that is still in place today. His beliefs and instruction—collectively known as the Rule of St. Benedict—still guide the practice hundreds of years later.

St. Benedict led by courageous example. If you are struggling with doubts or temptations in your job or your faith, let yourself be encouraged by St. Benedict. He rose above his many naysayers in order to carry out God's will. Many years later, we are discussing St. Benedict and his valuable contributions to the world.

St. Benedict is the patron saint of agricultural workers, cavers, civil engineers, coppersmiths, dying people, farmers, monks, and students.

St. Benedict demonstrated extreme strength every time he encountered evil. The devil visited him frequently in an attempt to turn him from God's light, but it never worked. If you are experiencing a seemingly impossible situation, remind yourself that temptation will arise repeatedly in all our lives. Sometimes we suffer the doubts and discouraging words of our contemporaries in the short term, even while we are doing work that will leave a lasting positive impression on the world in the long term.

When you successfully resist negative actions or destructive urges, take a moment to acknowledge it! Just like St. Benedict, you have a strong moral center and a well of great inner strength. Keep your heart open and your mind focused, and God will guide you to do the work that he put you here to do.

ST. BERNADETTE OF LOURDES

Think back on the time when you were a teenager. Perhaps, like many parents, yours were prone to minimizing the things that were a big deal to you during that period of life. When teens try to convince adults of something, it can often be an uphill battle!

This was exactly the dilemma that St. Bernadette of Lourdes faced. Born Marie-Bernarde Soubirous in 19th-century France, she came from an extremely humble and unremarkable background. She was the daughter of a miller, and the first of nine children. At the age of 14, she experienced a holy vision that would change her life.

One day, while she, a sister, and their friend were out gathering firewood near a grotto, Bernadette heard mysterious rustling. Suddenly, a brightly lit "small young lady" appeared out of nowhere! Bernadette reported the incident to her friend and the rest of her family, but they were unable to provide any explanation. In fact, her own mother expressed embarrassment about the incident, and she discouraged Bernadette from repeating the account of her experience. However, Bernadette was not deterred and stayed true to her beliefs.

Upon Bernadette's return to the grotto a few days later, she saw the apparition again. This time, Bernadette fell into a trance. Her friends tossed holy water and rocks in the general direction of the apparition, which caused it to disappear. When Bernadette saw the vision yet again on a subsequent trip, the figure requested that she return every day for the next two weeks.

The next two weeks of Bernadette's life are now known as *la Quinzaine sacrée*, or "the holy fortnight." This is because the vision appeared to Bernadette each and every day for the entire period. The clothing and adornments (white veil, blue girdle, and yellow rose on each foot) led people to speculate that the apparition was the Virgin Mary. Later—only after being repeatedly asked—the vision would identify itself to Bernadette as "the Immaculate Conception."

Now, if this incident happened in the modern day, it would probably play out the same way as it did in Bernadette's time. The story gained widespread news coverage, and the public was divided sharply between the believers and the skeptics.

Think of any recent news story and consider the strong reactions that people tend to have to stories about public figures. Now imagine how a 14-year-old girl with limited education might respond to a sudden wave of unwanted scrutiny and attention. Bernadette's accounts drew criticism, questions, and sometimes even accusations. Many people openly speculated about Bernadette's mental health, and called for her to be institutionalized!

Bernadette never wavered in her accounts, despite the backlash. During the holy fortnight, Bernadette reported that the vision told her to drink and wash with the water of the nearby spring, and to eat the herb that grew there as an act of penance. The following day, the springwater flowed clearly, even though previously it had been muddy. Shortly after that, the apparition revealed to Bernadette that a chapel should be built and a procession formed.

The incident gained so much publicity that the Catholic Church began an official canonical investigation. It concluded that Bernadette's claims were "worthy of belief." It is easy to think of this official ruling as a vindication of Bernadette's claims. However, all that publicity surely took a toll on her. Bernadette did not appreciate the attention the incident attracted, so she took the religious habit of a postulant and joined the Sisters of Charity in Nevers.

According to all accounts, Bernadette appreciated her time in Nevers. She was able to serve God in relative privacy, which must have been very welcome after the chaotic news coverage of her youth.

If you need a reminder of the simple power of righteousness, think of St. Bernadette! St. Bernadette was a woman who always sought to serve God, Jesus, and the Virgin Mary. She held a very humble view toward all the good that she caused, saying, "The Blessed Virgin used me as a broom to brush away the dust. When the job is done the broom is placed behind the door and stays there."

There are many miracles directly and indirectly attributed to St. Bernadette. The most prominent involves the incorrupt nature of Bernadette's own body—that is, her body was practically free from decomposition for each of the three times that it was exhumed. Other miracles involve the healing powers of the springwater by the grotto. The Lourdes Medical Bureau has recorded 69 cases involving cures that could be linked to the drinking of the springwater.

It is a rare person who enjoys living under the microscope of public opinion; rarer still is the person who can emerge from such relentless scrutiny without ill effects. The story of St. Bernadette reminds us that to tell the truth is not always easy, and that sometimes people will lash out if you tell them something they aren't ready to hear. To borrow a term from modern technology, sometimes we have to be the "early adopter" in matters of faith!

St. Bernadette is the patron saint of those suffering from bodily illness, shepherds, the poor, and people ridiculed for their faith. You can look to her example when you need to stay strong in your faith.

ST. CATHERINE OF ALEXANDRIA

St. Catherine of Alexandria was one of many saints who was persecuted for her Christianity in the 3rd and 4th centuries A.D. She lived in a time and place that was very inhospitable to Christians. As a virgin martyr, Catherine has a story that bears a striking similarity to that of many of her martyred contemporaries. She embraced her faith, was tortured for her beliefs, and was put to death because she refused to renounce her religion.

But St. Catherine stands out for her exceptional oratory skill. Highly educated and passionate about scholarship, she decided to become a Christian at only 14 years old when she saw a vision of Mary and the infant Jesus. Throughout her life, Catherine was a woman of unshakable virtue, committed to education.

When the Roman emperor Maxentius began a campaign of persecuting Christians, the bold and persuasive Catherine set off to visit the emperor in order to personally denounce his actions. Although she was only 18 at the time, she was filled with confidence. She wasn't thinking of the distinct possibility of being put to death for her boldness. All she could think of was her passion for her religion, and she couldn't help but to try to speak up and object to a practice that she knew was wrong.

Amazingly, when Maxentius saw Catherine, he arranged for 50 orators and philosophers to debate her. She was outnumbered and intimidated. But moved by the power of the Holy Spirit, young Catherine defended Christianity so passionately and so persuasively that a group of watching pagans converted on the spot. Unfortunately, the converts were immediately sentenced to death.

Catherine's fate was no better. Her rhetorical skill enraged the emperor! The persuasiveness of her arguments only made him feel more confused and intimidated. Maxentius sentenced Catherine to torture and imprisonment.

As we can see in the story of St. Catherine, sometimes even the most logical appeals fall on deaf ears. What do you do in these times? Should you lie low to avoid "rocking the boat"? Or should you get even louder, in the hopes of causing a change not just in your situation, but also in the world?

Catherine did the latter, of course. The emperor had hoped that her imprisonment and torture would break her spirit and cause her to disavow her beliefs. When this didn't happen, Maxentius made a final, last-ditch effort to "break her" by proposing marriage to her. Catherine calmly responded that she was married to Jesus Christ and that her virginity belonged to him.

This was the last straw. Maxentius commanded that Catherine be executed on the breaking wheel—a highly barbaric machine that caused a brutal and slow death through crushing a person's bones. However, when Catherine touched the wheel, it miraculously shattered. Because of this event, breaking wheels are also known as "Catherine wheels."

Ultimately, this miracle did not save Catherine. Frustrated once again, the emperor had her beheaded. According to one account, angels then carried her body to Mount Sinai, where a church and monastery was later established in her name.

Besides her shattering of the wheel, Catherine performed another miracle upon her martyrdom. When she was executed, she did not bleed; instead, a white milky fluid poured from her body. After her death and burial, her bones secreted a sacred oil with healing properties.

St. Catherine is the patron saint of craftsmen who work with a wheel, such as potters, wheelwrights, milliners, haberdashers, knife sharpeners, and spinners. She is also the patron saint of unmarried girls, apologists, educators, dying people, archivists, girls, lawyers, librarians, nurses, philosophers, preachers, scholars, schoolchildren, stenographers, and scribes.

In artwork, she is often pictured with a Catherine wheel, which is a powerful reminder of what she was able to accomplish by her faith.

As you confront the obstacles and opponents that may stand in your way, think of St. Catherine's bravery as she faced a gruesome fate. Consider the personal opposition she faced, too—a mob of courtly philosophers and a huge population of pagan nonbelievers. Yet she stood up for what she knew was right, unfailing in her certainty that God was on her side.

St. Catherine of Siena

Have you ever been in a situation where there were only two apparent options, but you didn't like either of them? You probably thought, *This can't be all there is!* Maybe you leaned toward one choice, but then wavered because it wasn't entirely what you wanted to do. There may have been a catch—a "but"—that discouraged you and deterred you from pursuing that option.

This familiar situation was exactly what St. Catherine of Siena faced. For most women of 14th-century Italy, the choices were clear: marry or become a nun. But St. Catherine was not most women; she chose to do neither. Instead, she devoted her life to religious service by joining a local Dominican tertiary, which was an organization that allowed her to serve God while continuing to live at home. St. Catherine led an exceptionally miraculous life, in which she experienced stigmata (marks or sensations corresponding to Christ's crucifixion wounds) and visions beginning at the age of five.

Catherine came from a large family—her parents had 25 children. A cheerful and easygoing child, Catherine still had to face the daily dramas that arose from having so many siblings. For example, when her older sister Bonaventura died when Catherine was only 16, her parents pressured her to marry her sister's widower—yikes! This idea was unappealing to Catherine for a couple of reasons. First, she had heard from her late sister herself that this man was controlling and unruly. More importantly, Catherine hadn't planned on getting married at all, thanks to her strong religious devotion.

Perhaps you can relate to Catherine's dilemma. Think of a time when you have been pressured to do something you don't want to do. If this incident involved family issues, then you probably experienced an added layer of guilt, sense of obligation, and confusion. Of course, nobody should ever be expected to throw away their most deeply held convictions simply to appease family.

In this situation, Catherine loved her parents and wanted to do right by her late sister's memory. At the same time, she held uncompromisingly strict religious beliefs and had dedicated her virginity to Jesus. She knew that her parents' vision for her life was incompatible with the work that she hoped to do.

This moment of trial only made Catherine feel stronger in her beliefs. She chopped off her hair in protest and started a hunger strike. She also perfected a new mental technique. Each time she fought with her family, she used a series of visualization exercises in order to calm her emotions and meditate on creating a positive outcome. As she explained it to her companion Raymond of Capua years later: "Build a cell inside your mind, from which you can never flee."

In this mental cell, she imagined her father as Jesus, her mother as the Blessed Virgin Mary, and her siblings as apostles. This allowed her to gain a much-needed distance from the situation, and she was able to hold her ground until her parents relented and stopped pushing marriage on her.

During this time, Catherine joined the Third Order of St. Dominic. It was a "day job," so to speak, as Catherine was able to return to her parents' home each night, where she lived among her large family in near-total silence and solitude.

Living in the family home provided Catherine with routine and continuity. Perhaps it was the reflective peace she enjoyed there that allowed her to have another great vision. When she was 21, Catherine famously experienced an intense encounter with Jesus. In this vision, he presented her with a ring made of his foreskin, which she accepted. Her acceptance symbolized her "mystical marriage" with Christ. This reaffirmed her virginity and her lifelong pursuit of religious work.

Catherine's vision marked a turning point: upon presenting her with the ring, Jesus asked Catherine to devote herself to serving the poor and the sick. Based on this request, Catherine set off to travel all over Italy, promoting causes of clergy reform, religious advocacy, and even political activism.

Catherine fasted often and had a contemplative and disciplined nature. She was so devoted to theology and doctrine that she was named a doctor of the church. Catherine of Siena is the patron saint of Italy and all of Europe, the United States, nurses, people ridiculed for their piety, the sick, and those placed in situations of sexual temptation. She is considered a powerful protector against fire, bodily ailments, and sickness.

Catherine was a bold woman who was never afraid to speak out. She proclaimed the truth wherever she went—whether at home, to her family; or out in the world, to powerful political figures. She had "the gift of tears," as Pope Benedict XVI described it, "an exquisite, profound sensitivity, a capacity for being moved and for tenderness." This made her observant and considerate.

If you are an emotional person, or prone to crying easily, do not be distressed. Your connection to your emotions makes you empathetic and understanding, just as St. Catherine was. Nourish your compassion for others!

ST. CECILIA

Music is powerful! The best tunes can capture and evoke a mood. Think of the waves of emotion that rush over you when you listen to different types of songs. Perhaps one makes you feel uplifted and joyful because of its peppy beat. Maybe another makes you feel moody and contemplative, as a talented singer inspires you to reflect on a universal truth.

Nobody knew the power of song better than St. Cecilia, who lived and was martyred in 2nd-century A.D. Rome. Her association with singing and instruments began after she loudly sang to glorify God at her own wedding. This was no ordinary wedding performance, however. Cecilia raised her voice in protest—she hadn't wanted to get married at all due to her sworn commitment to religious chastity.

We all have moments when we are pushed to act in a way that is inconsistent with our beliefs. In Cecilia's case, she was either unable or unwilling to fight the forces and pressures of her time. Young women back then were expected to get married, and opposition to that path was not accepted. Like many of the strong women who devoted themselves to God in that era, St. Cecilia felt she was the "bride of Jesus Christ," not of a pagan nobleman.

When Cecilia sang at her own wedding, she did it to honor God and to remind herself of who she was. On her wedding night, when her new husband, Valerian, attempted to consummate the marriage, Cecilia "sang" once more—though this time, she sang the praises of her religion.

She informed Valerian that an angel of God was with them both in the bedchamber, watching over her to protect her virginity. When Valerian expressed skepticism, Cecilia informed him that if he wanted to see the angel for himself, he should travel to the third mile marker on the Via Appia and be baptized by Pope Urban I.

To Valerian's credit—and as a testament to Cecilia's powers of persuasion—he did as she requested. Upon his return, he saw the angel standing over Cecilia, crowning her with a chaplet of roses and lilies. Valerian remained a Christian for the rest of his life, and he converted his brother Tiburtius as well.

Cecilia, Valerian, and Tiburtius were sentenced to death for being Christians. The prefect of the city ordered an especially cruel death for Cecilia: He locked her up in her own bathhouse and tried to suffocate her by closing all windows and cranking up the furnace. Cecilia stayed calm throughout several days, again singing her praise to the Lord during her ordeal. As a result, her body was unaffected by the heat, scalding steam, and flames.

Enraged, the prefect sent an executioner to kill her. Even though she was struck three times on the neck with a sword, she lived another few days—during which time she continued to offer her religious testament and counsel to visitors. Her delayed death also allowed her to make a request to the pope that her home be converted into a church.

Years later, when her remains were moved from a catacomb to the church that she requested (Santa Cecilia in Trastevere), they were found to be incorrupt. Indeed, the deceased St. Cecilia simply looked as though she was napping.

St. Cecilia was canonized before the church required miracles to be performed. Nevertheless, her awesome powers of converting people to Christianity, along with the circumstances of her death, certainly contain elements of the miraculous.

St. Cecilia was surely a visionary woman and a skilled persuader. She harnessed her quiet courage and inspiring passion in order to remain a virgin, married to a Christian, for the rest of her life.

Have you ever taken a bad situation and "talked your way out of it"? How were you able to use the powers of speech and logic to advance your cause? Perhaps you, like St. Cecilia, have been able to make a person change their mind completely based on the simple truth of your arguments! Look to her example whenever you doubt the power of a heartfelt testimonial.

Having used the power of song and her voice to spread the word of God and the love of Jesus, St. Cecilia is the patron saint of music, musicians, and poets. In artwork, she is often shown with instruments such as a flute, organ, harp, or violin. She is often depicted singing or wearing roses. Because of the crucial role of music in the church, and because of the pious example by which St. Cecilia led her life, she is one of the saints mentioned in the Canon of the Mass.

ST. CHRISTOPHER

In each stage of our life, we recognize different heroes, mentors, and idols. When we are children, perhaps we idolize someone in our family such as a parent or an older sibling. As we grow older, our idols may shift to match our views of what is "cool." We may start to greatly admire a musician, an astronaut, a celebrity, or a sports star. As adults, when we choose a path for ourselves and make progress toward our calling, our heroes and idols may become more like mentors and guides.

Have you ever had a hero surprise you? Maybe there was a time when your idol showed weakness, and you were reminded of their ability to fail. Perhaps your mentor got in trouble, and you realized that everyone has struggles. Sometimes the most shocking and hard-to-grasp thing about our heroes is that they are only human.

St. Christopher's conversion to Christianity was triggered by a powerful moment in which he came to understand the limitations of earthy kings as compared to Christ, the "king of kings."

Originally known as Reprobus, the man who became St. Christopher was tall and stern looking. By popular account, he was seven and a half feet tall, and he never smiled! A servant of the Canaanite king, he idolized his monarch and enjoyed his job, but he couldn't help but imagine there was something bigger out there.

One day Reprobus grew restless and departed his cozy post in search of "the greatest king there was." The first stop on his search was the court of a competing king, who Reprobus had heard was fiercer and more powerful than the king of Canaan. At first, that appeared to be true. But one day, when the name of the devil was spoken, this king crossed himself in fear. That episode caused Reprobus to see that even if this man was more powerful than the king of Canaan, there was something even more powerful than both of them.

Reprobus departed again, and he came across a the leader of a band of criminals who answered to the name of the devil. However, Reprobus was dismayed to see that even the "devil" was not fearless—the leader saw a cross on the road one day and took great pains to avoid it!

Finally, Reprobus was beginning to understand. The only thing more powerful than both anointed kings and lawless marauders was Christ. So Reprobus sought out a Christian hermit for advice. The hermit explained that in order to please Christ, Reprobus could either begin a life of fasting and prayer or take a job that would assist others. Reprobus had no desire to fast—he was a large and hungry man!—but he was intrigued by the idea of a life of service. He went to a dangerous river crossing and began using brute strength to carry people across to safety.

One day, in the course of this work, Reprobus was asked to carry a child across the river. *No problem*, he thought. This task would surely present no difficulty for a man of Reprobus's size! But as soon as Reprobus loaded the kid on his back, the tide rose and the child seemed to grow as heavy as lead. Reprobus struggled and barely survived the journey.

Once on the opposite bank, Reprobus demanded answers. What had just happened? The child announced that he was Christ. As Reprobus carried the child across, he felt the weight of the world's problems and its sinners. The child assured Reprobus that his work was noble and helpful and pleasing to Christ. Then, with that, the child disappeared. This was the episode that changed Reprobus into Christopher, a name that means "Christ-bearer."

Our understanding of St. Christopher is incomplete, and his story differs in some traditions. We do know that he falls into the saintly category of Christian martyrs. When Christopher traveled to Lycia in a time of widespread Christian persecution, he was brought before the local pagan king and called upon to make a sacrifice to the pagan gods. (This was a common form of public "test" in order to prove allegiance to pagan ideals.)

Not only did Christopher refuse to renounce his beliefs, but he also converted two onlookers to Christianity based on the strength of his appeals. The king was enraged, of course, and ordered that Christopher be executed. Due to Christopher's height, strength, and rock-solid faith, several execution attempts failed.

In fact, during the hour of his called-for execution, Christopher performed several miracles, including causing a dead branch to blossom and making loaves of bread multiply. These 11th-hour miracles moved several more onlookers to convert to Christianity. At last, Christopher was martyred, ending the earthly life of a man who would become an extremely popular saint.

While Christopher does not appear in the official canon of saints, he is widely known as a patron saint of travelers. He is also a patron saint of bachelors and gardeners, and a protector against storms, epilepsy, and toothache. In artwork, he is commonly depicted as a giant of a man with a small child (Christ) on his shoulder.

The tale of Christopher's conversion helps show us that the frustrations and stumbling blocks of our lives can often be moments of enlightenment and great clarity. The next time you find you have taken on a task that initially seemed straightforward but then morphed midstream into something more involved, think of Christopher bearing Christ across the river and emerging with renewed purpose and confidence in his mission. Likewise, sometimes what we think is a trial or a setback can turn out to be a valuable lesson, or a turning point, or a moment that strengthens our faith and religious development in the long run.

ST. CLARE OF ASSISI

St. Clare, designated as the Roman Catholic saint of television in 1958, lived and died in the 12th and 13th century. She promoted the idea of broadcast, in a general sense, years before the technology existed that gave rise to the televisions we use today. How is this possible?

St. Clare of Assisi was no ordinary woman. In many ways, she was ahead of her time. Renowned through the ages as a "miracle worker," this Italian saint contributed many revolutionary ideas to the practice of Christianity, particularly pertaining to Franciscan monastic life.

Born to a wealthy count and countess in Assisi, Clare demonstrated an early devotion to Christ. She performed numerous pilgrimages to Rome, Santiago de Compostela, and the Holy Land.

At age 18, Clare heard her contemporary and fellow countryman Francis of Assisi preach. She was moved to ask him for guidance on living according to his teachings. This sparked a lifelong friendship and spiritual partnership between the two. Later that year, Clare traveled to the chapel of Porziuncula to meet with Francis.

At Porziuncula, Clare furthered her commitment to an ascetic life by cutting her hair and donning the plain robe and veil of the monastery. Francis advised Clare to join the Benedictine convent of San Paulo, but at this time, Clare's parents became worried about their 18-year-old daughter's abrupt departure from home. Clare's father demanded that she return, but Clare clung tightly to the altar in protest and showed her shorn head in order to prove her seriousness about adopting a religious lifestyle.

Others were moved by the strength of Clare's commitment. Her sister Catarina followed her to a new nunnery in a more remote location in Subasio, where she adopted the name of Agnes.

Joined by a few more women, the group became known as the Poor Ladies of San Damiano, or the Poor Clares.

St. Clare and the Poor Ladies took the strictest vow of poverty, shunning the idea of maintaining possessions. United in their vows of simplicity, poverty, austerity, and seclusion, the Poor Clares demonstrated their religiosity by walking barefoot, sleeping on the ground, abstaining from meat, and observing near-total silence. When Pope Gregory IX offered them a special dispensation from their vow of poverty for practical reasons, Clare refused, stating: "I need to be absolved from my sins, but not from the obligation of following Christ."

Clare was humble, thoughtful, and always a protector. She would often get up in the middle of the night and tend to her sisters who had kicked off their blankets. In a widely commemorated moment, St. Clare protected her convent from a band of Saracen mercenaries by holding up a holy monstrance (a sacred vessel used in church service) as though it were a shield and praying over it. This caused the would-be invaders to flee.

Among the many miracles attributed to St. Clare, several occurred within her lifetime. The first was her protection of her convent in 1240, during which she held the attackers at bay by wielding her monstrance. She protected the convent from siege again several years later, when the troops of Vitalis d'Aversa attempted to breach the gates at Assisi. Once more, St. Clare moved others with her faith in God and deep devotion to the Eucharist, and the city was unharmed.

Another miracle occurred as St. Clare lay on her deathbed. On Christmas Eve, the year before she died, 58-year-old Clare yearned to attend Mass at the Basilica of St. Francis. But due to her weakness and infirmity, she was unable to leave her room. Despite the fact that her room was over a mile from the basilica, Clare saw the Mass projected on the wall of her room in such detail that she was able to name which friars had been present.

This early analogue of the television—the idea of images projected from a remote point, and reaching the world through the strength of their signal—is the inspirational metaphor that best describes the reach and impact of St. Clare's life of faithful Christian service.

The strength of Clare's passion is certainly impressive. Can you think of a time that you were offered riches or comforts, and yet you refused? This may not be a scenario that many of us can relate to. After all, we are not all called to take the vow of total poverty, or to live an austere life of silent reflection. We simply owe it to St. Clare to respect and understand her actions, and to draw inspiration from the discipline and vision that she always showed.

Due to her lifelong commitment to protecting others, St. Clare is the patron saint of goldsmiths, sufferers of eye disease, embroiderers, gilders, needleworkers, and of Santa Clara Pueblo. She is also associated with laundry, television, and good weather. St. Clare is often depicted in artwork with the monstrance she used to protect her convent, or with her pyx, lamp, or habit of the Poor Clares.

St. Dymphna

We've all clashed with a parent—this can be one of the most stressful conflicts of all. We hope that our parents have our best interests at heart, but they are only human. Sometimes they're afflicted with illness or confusion, or perhaps they are receiving bad counsel. What do we do in those situations? How do we find the strength to "rock the boat," and to do what is best not only for us but for them as well?

As a teenage virgin martyr, St. Dymphna experienced much hardship during her brief but eventful life. Her actions provide a powerful template for exemplary behavior in our most challenging moments. It is when our lives seem the most out of control and crazy that we most need to exercise our restraint and to show our faith in God.

Throughout Dympha's life, everyone commented on how much she resembled her mother—they were like mirror images of each other, both their beautiful faces and their strong Christian faiths. Her father was a pagan king, and she had a happy early childhood in 7th-century Ireland. But when Dymphna was only 14, the strong similarity between mother and daughter went from asset to liability. For in that year, Dymphna's mother died unexpectedly, and her father's mental health took a sharp decline in his grief.

Anguished and lonely, Dymphna's father, Damon, sought a second wife. Unfortunately, he held his late wife up as the unreachable ideal, swearing that his new bride should be just as beautiful and pure. After an exhaustive search around the kingdom proved fruitless, Damon set his sights inside his own home and turned to his daughter with indecent thoughts. In his delirious confusion, Damon decided that Dymphna exhibited all the wonderful traits that his late wife had—from her gentle heart to her lovely (and nearly identical) face.

Of course, this development was distressing for Dymphna. Prior to Dymphna's mother's death, the teenager had consecrated herself to Christ and taken a vow of chastity, so she was not interested in marriage in the first place. Worst of all, her father, who was supposed to protect her, was now actively pursuing her! So Dymphna fled the court with her confessor Father Gerebernus, two faithful servants, and the king's fool. They took refuge near a shrine dedicated to St. Martin of Tours, in a town called Gheel, in a region corresponding to present-day Belgium.

In Gheel, Dymphna devoted herself to helping the poor and sick. She used some of the money she had brought from home to build a hospice. Unfortunately, the coins she used allowed her father to trace her whereabouts, and he sent his men after her.

When Damon and his men found Dymphna and her crew, he tried to convince his daughter to return to Ireland with him. In the skirmish that ensued, Damon murdered Father Gerebernus. With Dymphna's confessor now dead, Damon pleaded once more with his daughter to return home with him as his wife. He promised safety, prestige, and money—things that had no strong pull on his purehearted Christian daughter.

Dymphna bravely stated that she would rather die than break the vow of chastity she had made to God. Out of spiteful rage at this complete rejection, Damon drew his sword and decapitated his own daughter.

Despite her earthly suffering, Dymphna modeled true faith and strength of character. Sadly, in her case, the phrase "No good deed goes unpunished" applies, as it was her almsgiving that led her father to her and, ultimately, to her death at the age of 15.

Dymphna is the patron saint of runaways and victims of incest. She is recognized for many miracles related to the healing of the chronically ill, and for the alleviation of suffering for those afflicted with mental, emotional, and nervous disorders. Gheel, the town where St. Dymphna died, is home to her remains and to a church bearing her name. It is also a popular pilgrimage site for those struggling with nervous distress. According to Bollandist scholars (those who study saints), St. Dymphna has interceded miraculously on behalf of many people who were insane or institutionalized, earning her the nickname "miracle worker."

In art, Dymphna is often depicted with a crown, sword, lily, and lamp—objects that reinforce her purity, her strong morality, and the clear direction she always had for herself. If you are feeling pressured, let yourself be guided by the grace that St. Dymphna showed, even when she faced her greatest trials!

.

ST. FAUSTINA KOWALSKA

Do you have a favorite painting? What about a favorite religious image? The beautiful iconography in churches, shrines, and other holy sites provide us with vivid reminders of the power of God's love.

If you have been moved by a particularly striking image of Jesus, you may be touched by the story of the virgin mystic St. Faustina Kowalska, also known as the "Apostle of Divine Mercy." Her life in early 20th-century Poland was not an easy one, as she faced poverty and chronic illness. She was drawn to record—and moved to share—her specific and powerful vision of the Divine Mercy of Jesus, even though she was continually met with skepticism by others. She wrote extensively on the topic, and her handwritten diary was turned into a 700-page published devotional called *The Diary of St. Maria Faustina Kowalska: Divine Mercy in Her Soul*.

Faustina experienced her first divine vision, of a suffering Jesus, at the age of 19, This episode kicked off the series of events that saw Faustina depart her hometown and her family life in search of a convent. She met many obstacles along the way, due to her poverty and lack of family connections, but Faustina persisted. When she was given the offer to join a convent if she could pay for her habit, Faustina worked as a housemaid to raise the funds.

Over the years, Faustina received many visions of Jesus and shared the contents of these apparitions with her teachers. However, she was not always favored with support: Faustina's own mentor, Father Michael Sopocko, ordered that she undergo a complete psychological evaluation when she told him of her conversations with Jesus. (Faustina was deemed to be of sound mind.)

In one of Faustina's conversations with Jesus, she learned that she was called to spread the image of Divine Mercy to all of the world. According to her diary, Jesus told her: "I promise that the soul that will venerate this image will not perish. I also promise victory over enemies already here on Earth, especially at the hour of death. I myself will defend it as my own glory."

Upon hearing this instruction, Faustina was clear on her divine direction. She immediately tried to paint the image of Divine Mercy that had appeared so vividly to her in her visions, and which was described by Jesus himself. She found herself unable to do the work justice, as she had no formal artistic training. Instead, St. Faustina commissioned Eugeniusz Kazimirowski to paint the image now known around the world: Jesus, clad in white, with his right hand raised in blessing and his left hand pointing down. From Jesus's left hand, two rays shoot forth—a red ray (for the blood of Christ) and a white ray (for the water, which justifies souls). The bottom contains an inscription, which Faustina was also directed to include: JESUS, I TRUST IN YOU.

Like the many chaste young women of the Church who were blessed with lifelong mystic episodes, Faustina had her fair share of contemporary detractors. Some openly expressed doubt about her deep and divine connection with Jesus. Although Faustina felt called to spread the image of Divine Mercy and to be the founder of a new contemplative religious congregation associated with the idea, her visions were met with objections from all the superiors of her order.

When her mission to found the congregation of Divine Mercy hit its final roadblock, Jesus told St. Faustina: "My daughter, do whatever is within your power to spread devotion to My Divine Mercy. I will make up for what you lack."

St. Faustina endured many years of physical discomfort due to her failing health before tuberculosis finally claimed her life.

Are you performing a hard task in a difficult time? Sometimes, we are called to do important work—but in an environment where our work will not be immediately appreciated. You may have worked tirelessly toward a goal, only to have to abandon your mission because of outside factors. Always remember that when your intentions are true but your objectives cannot be completed, Jesus is standing by to help "make up for what you lack"!

Know that you are not alone. You are in the noble company of Faustina, the patron saint of mercy and of her hometown of Łódz, and all the "suffering saints" who also walked a hard road! Their temporary discomfort on earth could never compare to the ecstasy that they felt in prayer, not to mention the glory that they received upon being reunited with God.

If you are struggling in your faith and eager to be bathed in the comforting glow of God's light, St. Faustina's "Divine Mercy" images and writings can serve as a powerful reminder. Enjoy the painting of Jesus that she commissioned and those that she inspired. Take comfort in the simple sentiment expressed at the bottom of all of St. Faustina's Divine Mercy depictions: *Jesus, I trust in You!*

ST. FLORIAN

Fire. It has entered our language and symbolic imagination as a sign of destruction—and of faith.

For example, think of a "blaze" that you have tried to fight. It could be literal, but most likely it is figurative—for example, a massive, widespread problem that you have had trouble controlling or extinguishing. Think of how this blaze has spread out to the different areas of your life, affecting your ability to lead the happy and calm existence that we all seek.

One holy man who knew about fire—and the fires of faith, with all its conflicts and complications—was St. Florian. Born in Cetium (present-day Austria), a territory of Rome, in A.D. 250, Florian quickly exhibited the discipline and leadership skills that are ideal for a military career.

After enlisting, Florian rose to the level of commander of the imperial army of Noricum (a Roman province). This position came with a political element. Florian was charged not only with performing military operations but also with enforcing the Roman emperor's rules and beliefs on a local level. In the years that followed, that tension between his religious beliefs and the emperor's commands set off the chain of events that led to Florian's martyrdom.

Separate from his army duties, Florian was also the leader of local fire brigades. He trained his fellow soldiers in the art of firefighting. He determined that soldiers were perfect for fulfilling this role thanks to their peak physical fitness, tactical skill, and extreme discipline.

St. Florian was a deeply religious man, secure in his Christian convictions. But he lived during an era of widespread Christian persecution, and this fact caused a huge problem due to Florian's high military rank. According to the Diocletianic Edict of 303, Christians had no legal rights in Rome and were ordered to comply with traditional Roman religious practices. As a matter of course, Roman political leaders would "test" their subjects' allegiance to Roman pagan traditions by demanding on-the-spot sacrifices and other non-Christian rites.

As a military officer, Florian was entrusted with enforcing the practice of Roman religion over Christianity in his local jurisdiction. However, he did not comply. When the governer, Aquilinus, visited to investigate the noncompliance, he saw the level of Florian's commitment and sentenced him to be burned at the stake.

Even with extensive firsthand experience with the the terror wrought by fire, Florian looked at his immolation pyre and boldly proclaimed, thanks to the depth of his commitment to Christ: "I will climb to heaven on the flames!"

Aquilinus's men weren't sure whether to believe this, yet Florian's proclamation scared them. They decided to instead torture him and then tie a millstone around his neck and drown him in the nearby Enns River. After his body was buried at a nearby Augustinian monastery, a woman named Valeria experienced a vision of Florian in which he asked that his remains be moved to a different location.

Among the miracles attributed to St. Florian, perhaps the best known is an episode in which he extinguished a huge blaze with a small bucket of water alone. What a powerful image and example! Here was a man who never renounced his strong faith, despite the "inferno" that he faced daily as a Christian man living in a very anti-Christian time in history.

Even though we may feel we are facing an uphill battle—like we are trying to fight a huge fire with only a few drops of water—there is always reason to keep the faith. For through God, even our greatest obstacles can be tamed when we put our faith first, and act according to our Christian hearts.

St. Florian is extremely popular in Central Europe, and he is the patron saint of Kraków, Poland, and of Linz, Austria. He is also the patron saint of chimney sweeps, firefighters, and soap boilers. His likeness is often seen at firehouses, and the word *Florian* is the call sign for fire stations and fire trucks in Germany and Austria. In many regions of Bavaria and Austria, families name a male child Florian in order to secure protection against house fires.

St. Florian is often depicted in stained-glass windows, in illuminated manuscripts, and in architectural relief sculptures and statues. In his many depictions, St. Florian is often shown carrying a lance (due to his military connection), beside a tub (due to the power of water against fire, and his miracles), and with a millstone (as a reminder of the last-ditch execution method that his tormentors had to employ after he was shown to be fearless when facing fire).

ST. FRANCIS OF ASSISI

Have you ever been called to do something, but felt too scared to do it right away? Sometimes we need time and a little perspective to rise to the occasion. That's what happened to St. Francis of Assisi, the founder of the Franciscan order.

Nearly 800 years after his death, St. Francis remains one of the most important religious figures in history. But when Francis was a young man trying to navigate his education and career, it certainly didn't feel that way to him. Growing up, all he felt was extreme confusion and internal conflict. He may have made his share of youthful mistakes, but when the time was right, he summoned an inner strength and embraced God with complete commitment.

The man who would become St. Francis of Assisi was originally named Giovanni di Bernardone. His parents were wealthy Italians, and his father, Pietro, was a highly successful traveling silk merchant. Pietro traveled so often, in fact, that he was out of the country when St. Francis was born.

Upon returning from abroad, Pietro learned that his new son had been baptized as Giovanni, after St. John the Baptist. Pietro was furious! He disliked this religious connection and so chose instead to call the new baby Francesco, or Francis for short. The name, meaning "the Frenchman," was a reflection of Pietro's love of travel and the importance he placed on gaining worldwide commercial success. In Pietro's eyes, making money was far more important than demonstrating piety.

Throughout his childhood and adolescence, Francis continued to be influenced by his parents and their beliefs. He enjoyed a wealthy upbringing and he drank, partied, and broke curfew as a teenager. He had a reputation for being charming, suave, and a bit reckless. Later, he served in the military, as was common for men of his station.

As he traveled the world as a soldier, Francis became exposed to new ideas that intrigued him. Initially, becoming a knight appealed to him because the life of a war hero seemed so glamorous. While touring with the armed forces, Francis encountered many unfamiliar situations that forced him to confront his beliefs.

The culmination of these unfamiliar situations came when Francis was captured by the enemy and forced to serve as a prisoner of war. What a shock to the system! Here was a pampered young man whose experiences had in no way prepared him for the true horrors of war. It wasn't until after a year of imprisonment—as well as the payment of a hefty ransom fee by Francis's parents—that he was finally released.

Physically, Francis's transformation was clear to see. The long imprisonment had weakened his body dramatically. And as for his spiritual transformation? Well, Francis returned from that underground cell forever changed.

Francis emerged with a newfound motivation to devote his life to work that truly mattered to him. He threw himself wholeheartedly into prayer, reflection, and tending toward the sick and poor. He devoted all his time and energy to helping groups like the lepers, who were largely ignored or mistreated by others.

This seemingly dramatic shift from soldier to religious devotee shocked Francis's parents. His father expected him to take over the family silk trade, and this newfound interest in religion clashed with that hope. The final straw in the growing tension with his parents came after Francis received a mystical vision of Jesus Christ. The Icon of Christ Crucified spoke directly to Francis and urged him to "fix my church."

Naturally, Francis assumed Jesus meant "church" as in a physical building. So he immediately took money from his wealthy father and donated it to the local church, which was indeed in physical disrepair. Pietro, however, was furious. He dragged his son to court, where the Bishop of Assisi ordered Francis to repay the money to his father. In response, Francis renounced his inheritance—and therefore his family—and resolved to live as a beggar with no possessions.

He was inspired by a sermon he had recently heard, quoting Matthew 10:9, where Jesus urges his followers to go forth and tell others that the Kingdom of Heaven was upon them, and that followers should bring nothing of value for the journey. No money, no jewelry—not even a walking stick or shoes!

Through years of travel and teaching, St. Francis inspired many with his simple humility, his embrace of suffering, and his generosity toward others. He considered all people to be his "brothers and sisters," and many miracles are attributed to him. He spent lots of time around people with terminal diseases and was known to heal lepers, people suffering from malaria, and those afflicted with highly communicable diseases like meningitis.

St. Francis's lifelong compassion for the defenseless and the vulnerable aligns with his love for animals and connection with nature. He taught that humans were not to harm animals, and that we should step in and help them whenever possible. He was known to be comfortable with all kinds of animals. There is a story of him preaching to a flock of birds, who listened peacefully, and one of him taming a vicious wolf that had been attacking humans and animals.

St. Francis is the patron saint of Italy, animals, the environment, silk merchants, and San Francisco, California. You can recall his example when you hope to be reminded of the needy and when you want to renew your faith and hope.

Like Francis's newfound calling after serving as a prisoner of war, sometimes it can take a dramatic moment to push us toward our destiny! When we respond to stressful situations, our true selves emerge. Don't be surprised if you discover during times of trouble that you're stronger than you thought you were.

St. Gemma Galgani

Are you suffering from afflictions, either physical or mental? Each of us walks this earth knowing all sorts of pain. There are those among us who suffer greatly, courageously battling the great bodily pain of illness or injury. There are still others who seem to lead "charmed" lives, rich in health and abundance—but even these people must face the pain of heartache, disappointment, or spiritual conflict.

St. Gemma Galgani, who lived in the late 19th century, also suffered a barrage of earthly setbacks in her 25 years of life. Both her parents died, she endured painful chronic illness, and she was the target of near-constant scrutiny and ridicule. Yet after each trial she faced, she emerged happier, stronger, and surer of her deep devotion to Christ. She was a woman who suffered greatly, but gladly—a "victim soul," as some might term it. Her connection to God and her work in his service make her an excellent model when we seek inspiration for how to deal with the disappointments and challenges of life.

St. Gemma Galgani was a woman of extremes. The revered Italian saint earned the nicknames "Daughter of Passion" and "Passionate Flower" due to her deep commitment to an imitation of Jesus Christ's suffering during the Passion. Gemma valued her relationship with Jesus highly, and she sought to base her life as closely as possible on his example.

Gemma moved through her life demonstrating a selfless desire to suffer for others. The fifth of eight children, she was forced to accept caregiver roles early on when several of her family members—including her mother, her father, and two siblings—died from tuberculosis. By age 18, Gemma was both orphan and foster parent to her remaining siblings. This was one of the many challenges that young Gemma faced, which she responded to with a renewed passion for God.

A lifelong devotee of Christ, Gemma wrote extensively in her journals of a desire to "suffer everything" as expiation for her sins. Despite the physical pain from meningitis and other maladies, Gemma denied herself earthly comforts as an expression of her desire to understand God better. She hoped to grow closer to Jesus through extensive study, prayer, and soul-searching.

In answer to Gemma's deep devotion, Jesus revealed himself to her through visions, ecstasies, and stigmata. Her mystical episodes grew more intense when she was in the final throes of a tuberculosis infection that would prove fatal. In the words of one of the nursing sisters who cared for St. Gemma on her deathbed: "We have cared for a good many sick people, but we have never seen anything like this."

Many were moved by Gemma's passionate example, but she had her detractors, too. (The skepticism and derision directed toward Gemma—much of which occurred even while she was still alive—can be seen as another way she suffered for her faith.) Even her own sister Angelina was one; her mockery and attempts to profit off Gemma caused her to be ruled unfit to testify during Gemma's canonization trial.

Whatever your "pain," think of St. Gemma. Here was a woman who not only embraced her own pain, but also asked to take on the suffering of others. Even if we are not ready to ask that God put "extra" suffering on our plates at this point—most of us aren't like St. Gemma!—we may still draw an important lesson from her humility and willingness to offer up her life as a personal sacrifice to God.

St. Gemma Galgani is the patron saint of students (due to the way she excelled in her studies, even in illness), headache and migraine sufferers, pharmacists, paratroopers and parachutists, and the poor and unemployed. All of St. Gemma's recognized miracles involve cures and healing—including her healing of a woman's stomach cancer and her cure of a case of acute meningitis.

St. Gemma is often represented with her Passionist robe, with flowers such as lilies or roses, with her stigmata, and with the heavenward gaze that symbolizes a life spent completely focused on God.

ST. GERARD

"I see in my neighbor the Person of Jesus Christ." This simple and powerful quotation is attributed to St. Gerard Majella of Naples, a miracle worker who lived in the 18th century and demonstrated the selflessness and empathy indicated by this quote—all while wrestling with illness and malicious gossip. When you face your own trials and discomforts, does it increase or decrease your faith in God? Does it add to or detract from your love for your fellow man?

The youngest of five children, Gerard was only 12 when his father died. Times were dire, and the six remaining members of the Majella family faced extreme poverty and hardship. Gerard and his siblings were forced to enter the workforce to support the family.

Gerard went to his uncle's tailor shop in order to learn the family trade. That job ended badly when Gerard observed the foreman at the shop abusing his power; the foreman resigned, leaving him without a teacher. Gerard then began an apprenticeship with the local bishop of Lacedonia. When the bishop died, Gerard went back to tailoring. As he earned his living, he began the habit of dividing his earnings three ways: one part to his mother, one part to the poor, and one part as an offering to the souls in purgatory.

At 23, St. Gerard desired to join the Capuchin monastery in Muro, but his application was rejected twice. He was told that his subpar health made him a poor candidate for the physical demands of the order. Undaunted, Gerard applied to and was accepted by the Redemptorists, also known as the Congregation of the Most Holy Redeemer at Scala. This missionary order devoted itself to "preaching the word of God to the poor"—a perfect match for Gerard's growing charitable tendencies. He took vows of poverty, chastity, and obedience, and dedicated himself to "do the will of God."

As Redemptorist, Gerard was called on to take many odd jobs, to be a jack-of-all-trades. His time in the order included stints as tailor, porter, cook, carpenter, gardener, sacristan, and clerk of works on the new buildings of Caposele, Italy, where he lived.

But as Gerard began to make a name for himself through his diverse talents and tireless work ethic, he was the target of a pernicious accusation. An acquaintance of his named Neria claimed that Gerard had inappropriate relations with a young woman. The allegation sparked an inquiry, at which time Alphonsus Liguori, the founder of the Redemptorists himself, investigated the claims. Later, the young lady recanted, formally clearing Gerard of the charges.

Imagine what Gerard must have felt at this time! Have you ever worked tirelessly, trying to do good, while feeling that others doubted your motives? These moments can almost be considered trials, as we are called to rise above the very understandable human emotions that such injustices inspire. Gerard certainly did. He was determined not to let an unfortunate incident mar the purity and power of his Christian mission.

After six years of devout service in his religious orders, Gerard became very ill with tuberculosis. Even in his weakened state, his faith never wavered. His one request was to place the following words upon his door: "Here the will of God is done, as God wills, and as long as God wills." Although his health miraculously improved afterward, he became ill again only a month later and passed away at the age of 29.

As a healer and mystic, Gerard is credited with performing numerous miracles. These include an episode in which he revived a boy who had fallen from a high cliff, one in which he rid a poor farmer's field of mice that were destroying the crops, and many tales of multiplying bread to feed the poor.

The final miracle officially attributed to Gerard is also the origin of his reputation for protecting pregnant women. One day, while walking by a young girl, Gerard unwittingly dropped his handkerchief. She picked it up, held on to it for a while, then set out to return it to its rightful owner. When the girl finally found

Gerard and offered his lost item back, Gerard declined, telling her, "You may need it someday."

Years later, after Gerard had passed, the same woman was suffering a troubled labor with her first child. She nearly lost her baby, but upon reaching for Gerard's old handkerchief, the pain subsided and she gave birth to a healthy baby.

In his short life, St. Gerard displayed certain mystical capacities, including gifts of levitation, bilocation, and the power to intuitively "read souls." All these traits indicate the strong connection that Gerard shared with the souls of both other people and Jesus Christ. Widely known as "The Patron of Mothers," St. Gerard is the patron saint of motherhood, children (including the unborn), childbirth, falsely accused people, good confessions, lay brothers, and Muro Lucano, Italy.

St. Gerard is often depicted in a simple manner, carrying a cross or perhaps with a skull. It is said that he kept a skull and crossbones on his desk as a reminder that his life on earth would not be long, and that he would soon face judgment before God.

St. Hildegard of Bingen

Through our thoughts and our actions, we may try to "see" God's influence in the world around us. We can do this literally, by appreciating the lovely things that are in our field of vision. For example, perhaps looking at a beautiful flower reminds us of the complexity and masterful handiwork of divine creations. Similarly, we may try to "hear" God's power, too—from the inspiration of a wonderfully composed piece of music to the miraculous joy of a newborn baby's cry.

Now imagine seeking God's influence through every sense, every day. With a little creativity, perhaps we can consider how we might see, hear, taste, smell, and touch the divine. (It's probably a bit more of a stretch than when we imagined just seeing and hearing God's influence!) Now that you have considered this perspective, you know a little more about the worldview of St. Hildegard of Bingen.

A learned saint and Doctor of the Church, Hildegard lived a long and influential life in 12th-century Germany. She wrote hundreds of letters and published visionary and helpful books on a wide range of subjects. She tackled topics of divinity, nutrition, Christian lifestyle, nature, and more.

Hildegard wore many hats in her eight decades of life—writer, philosopher, musical composer, Christian mystic, healer, Benedictine abbess. She even invented an entire language, the Lingua Ignota, which she used to describe her mystical encounters. But her most popular nickname—Sibyl of the Rhine—provides the biggest window onto her miraculous gifts as a seer.

Hildegard had her first divine vision when she was only three years old. In fact, she didn't even know what was happening when she experienced it. A couple of years later, when the episodes became a more regular occurrence, Hildegard adopted the term *visio* in an attempt to name a phenomenon that she knew was not universal.

Visions and close communion with God became a lifelong occurrence for Hildegard. However, Hildegard was so hesitant to share her experience with others that she told only one person of her visions, her aunt and spiritual confessor, Jutta. When Hildegard was 42, God finally told her to write down everything she saw and heard during the episodes.

Initially, the divine command made Hildegard feel physically sick with worry. Why would she feel so apprehensive? Well, as a prudent and learned woman, she understood that "out of the box" experiences were not always welcomed in 12th-century theology! But as she wrote in *Scivias* (Know the Ways), her first published theological text: "But I, though I saw and heard these things, refused to write for a long time through doubt and bad opinion."

Finally, she overcame her reluctance. Hildegard wrote about all that she saw, felt, heard, smelled, and tasted of God, as she experienced it. Her accounts were so convincing that in 1148, Pope Eugenius granted papal approval to document Hildegard's visions as revelations from the Holy Spirit.

Hildegard was not martyred. She lived to the age of 81, a long life as far as saints are concerned. She saw visions of God, and when she reported them, they were almost immediately accepted and corroborated.

Consider the mystics who lived in other times, and in other political environments. Sharing private visions does not always end so well! Many of the men and women of different eras who saw God in a similar manner were met with skepticism or worse.

What does this tell us about the impact of the times we live in? We can compare all the saints who were blessed with divine visions, and their stories can seem remarkably similar. But one saint in one era may have been celebrated as a philosopher, while another saint from a different period may have been accused of apostasy and put to death.

(To be fair, Hildegard did indeed have her detractors. Some doubted that a woman should be the one "chosen" to receive direct messages and visions from God. Still others claimed that her powerful prophetic episodes were probably just migraines!)

If you feel that your gifts or your experiences are being minimized or ignored, do not despair! Sometimes it takes only a shift in perspective, or in the prevailing climate of the times, for everything to change.

Interestingly, St. Hildegard is not explicitly the patron saint of anything. But it's not hard to find inspiration and motivation by examining her remarkable accomplishments. She was one of the first great German mystics, a poet, and a prophet. She also had a love for studying nutrition, writing recipes, and baking. Her most famous recipe, for "Cookies of Joy," called for wholesome ingredients. Eating the cookies was said to "reduce the bad humors, enrich the blood, and fortify the nerves."

She promoted the consumption of certain foods (for example, spelt, chestnuts, chickpeas, grass-fed animals, and vegetables) and the avoidance of others (sausage and refined sugar, for instance). The surprisingly "modern" nature of Hildegard's dietary recommendations from the 12th century only underscore the timelessness of her wise teaching.

Look to her fine example as you pursue knowledge, moderation, and strength through God!

St. Joan of Arc

Perhaps no saint captures the modern imagination more vividly and universally than Joan of Arc. Also known as the "Maid of Orléans," this teenage martyr is credited with directly and indirectly helping France to achieve incredibly important military victories—despite the fact that she had no martial training herself.

Joan, or Jeanne, was born in 1412 in a climate of extreme political instability in France. At the time, France was locked in a long and deadly conflict with England that later came to be known as the Hundred Years' War. In 1420, France's Dauphin (crown prince) Charles of Valois was disinherited and dethroned due to a treaty that England, which was winning the war, forced France to sign. From that moment, King Henry V ruled both England and France, and the situation was both tenuous and deeply demoralizing to the French.

Around this time, 13-year-old Joan began experiencing visions of saints. According to her own account, Joan was visited by St. Michael, St. Catherine, and St. Margaret, who told her that they were sent by God himself. They had a hugely important message to deliver to the teenager: Joan was to drive the English invaders out of France and deliver the Dauphin to Reims for his coronation.

What a responsibility God placed on young Joan's shoulders! Can you think of a time that you've been called to do something seemingly impossible? What was your response when you understood what was being asked of you?

Joan's response was action. She lived in a dire and desperate time; even as a child, she understood how much her fellow countrymen suffered during this bitter war. So at the age of 16, Joan began her important journey.

Joan's first stop was Vaucouleurs, a stronghold for supporters of the Dauphin. She met with a frosty reception. Upon telling the local magistrate of her mission, he practically laughed in her face.

But based on the power of her charisma and the single-minded-ness of her spirit, Joan won other followers on the road. Many had heard a popular prophecy that predicted that a virgin would save France, and Joan appeared to fit this bill.

Thanks to the pleas of this growing band of supporters, Joan finally changed the mind of the dubious magistrate. She cut her hair and wore men's clothing in order to cross undetected through enemy territory. Once she gained an audience with the Dauphin, Joan made her request: She wanted him to give her an army, which she would lead to Orléans in order to fight the English. Amazingly, the Dauphin agreed.

Talk about brave! Joan appeared fearless not only in her will-ingness to enter the battlefield but also in her readiness to speak directly to one of the most powerful figures in France. Joan of Arc showed confidence in the divinity of her mission. And as is so often the case, her faith was contagious. Her efforts were bolstered further by the French townspeople who came to see Joan as the answer to prophecies and prayers.

Joan led the battalion heroically, and the French claimed a victory over their English foe. Just as had been foretold in her saintly vision, Joan of Arc led the Dauphin through enemy terri-tory to Reims, where he was coronated in 1429.

After a series of further military triumphs, Joan of Arc was captured in hostile territory in 1430. Now Joan's widely known successes became a liability for her. Her capture provided the opportunity for her naysayers to put her on a highly publicized trial, which became something of a circus, in an English-backed church court in Rouen, Normandy. Joan was called to answer for her alleged heresy, witchcraft, and cross-dressing. All told, there were 70 charges against her.

Joan was imprisoned under terrible conditions for over a year. Seeing no other alternative, she signed a confession in 1431 that denied her religious visions.

It can be tempting to pity the teenage Joan, locked away under squalid conditions as a prisoner of war. At the same time, take heart in her courageous example. She came from a strong religious background, and she drew comfort from her faith. There's little wonder that she turned to God and prayer more than ever during the time of her wretched captivity.

The persecution would continue. A few days after Joan signed her confession, she was again charged with cross-dressing. This charge may have been true: According to contemporary accounts, prison was a dangerous and unpoliced place, and women were in great danger of being assaulted. Joan may have worn military garb in prison rather than a loose dress, as a layer of protection from rape.

For her supposed crimes of heresy and "monstrous dress," Joan was sentenced to be burned at the stake at the tender age of 19. Her canonization took place more than 500 years later, by Pope Benedict XV in 1920.

St. Joan led a heroic and inspiring life. But if you examine the particulars of her persecution, it's easy to become disgusted and discouraged with the injustices of her time. Joan's forced confession is a situation that many of us can relate to. With our hands tied, so to speak, sometimes we have to take actions that we don't agree with. This human element perhaps explains her enduring popularity. She was a martyr, in both the Christian and the colloquial sense of the word.

Due to her suffering, and thanks to the strong role of divine guidance in Joan's life, she is the patron saint of soldiers, prisoners, people ridiculed for their piety, and France. In art, she is usually depicted as a young, bareheaded girl in armor, often carrying a sword, lance, or banner.

ST. JOHN OF THE CROSS

What makes you feel the love of God most—trials or triumphs?

This is a question that St. John of the Cross grappled with his entire life. A fascinating figure, this 16th-century Spanish saint was a mystic poet, a Carmelite friar, a Doctor of the Church, and a priest. (Many have heard of his popular poetic work, "Dark Night of the Soul," without knowing of this saint.) Rife with contradictions and opposing theories, his varied background caused him to have a philosophical and intellectual bent while remaining very strong in his faith.

St. John was born Juan de Yepes y Álvarez to an "odd couple" of sorts: His father, Gonzalo, was a successful accountant who was born into privilege, while his mother, Catalina, was a poor orphan who sometimes worked as a weaver. Upon the marriage of the two, Gonzalo's family disowned him, setting off a chain of events that led to poverty and instability for Gonzalo, Catalina, and eventually their three children.

Juan lived a life that was initially harsh. Gonzalo died when Juan was only three. And then things became so dire that Juan's older brother Luis died soon after—likely due to malnutrition caused by the family's ensuing poverty.

For some people, an extremely tough childhood like this would cause them to seek comfort and stability through whatever means possible. But Juan turned to religion and, as demonstrated by his full chosen name, embraced suffering. He lived a life filled with trials and discomforts, yet even so, he sought to take on more.

Juan's religious career began in 1563, when he entered the Carmelite order and took the name John of St. Matthias. He was ordained as a priest in 1567 and set his sights on joining the strict Carthusian order, which appealed to him due to its emphasis on solitude and total silence. But a life of silence and solitude was not to be his path.

During a trip to Medina del Campo, John encountered Teresa of Jesus (who later became St. Teresa of Ávila). Teresa was a charismatic Carmelite nun, and she had a strong vision of resuming observance of the Carmelite "Primitive Rule" of 1209. The Primitive Rule prescribed, among other things, that friars spend their time evangelizing to the local population. Nuns and friars alike were to go barefoot, or "discalced"—just as they always had from the creation of the Primitive Rule up until 1432, when this detail of the rule was relaxed.

Suddenly, John faced a crossroads. Would he join the silent, traditional Carthusian order he had planned on, or would he follow the persuasive Sister Teresa, with her powerful vision for reform?

For John, the answer was clear. Just as with everything else in his life, he sought to take the hard path, not the easy one. In this situation, the added upside of revitalizing his religious practice proved to be a particularly strong draw. And so John set out with Friar Antonio de Jesús de Heredia to go to a derelict house at Duruelo to found the very first monastery of the Discalced Carmelites, after Teresa's principles. At this stage in his life, John took the name John of the Cross. He chose it in order to remind himself of the suffering of Jesus, and to push himself to follow the extreme selflessness and discipline of Christ's example.

While things went well at first with Teresa and John's reform campaign, simmering intermonastic tensions came to a head in December 1577. Upset over what they saw as favored treatment, a group of Carmelites broke into John's home in Ávila and carried him off to the main house of the order. They made him stand trial for the alleged crime of disobeying the ordinances of Piacenza.

Despite John's vigorous defenses, he was found guilty and sentenced to a harsh existence in a monastery jail. His imprisonment included weekly public lashings, solitary confinement in a 10-foot-by-6-foot cell, and a very meager diet of water, bread, and fish scraps.

While some people might endure such a painful incarceration with defeat, John of the Cross took it in stride. As he wrote: "Where there is no love, put love—and you will find love." To that end, he used the time to write his famous poem "Spiritual Canticle," as well as many others. He accomplished this by writing on paper that a friar snuck under his cell doors.

After nine months, John was able to escape his prison cell and rejoin Teresa in Toledo. Until his death in 1591, he continued supporting the Discalced Carmelites, traveling, and establishing new houses across Spain.

St. John of the Cross highly valued suffering, and he was intimately familiar with its extremes. He is the patron saint of contemplatives, mystical theology and mystics, and Spanish poets. St. John is credited with several miracles of healing, including ridding a nun of palsy.

St. John of the Cross led a highly spiritual life that was often severely lacking in creature comforts. Born into poverty, he selflessly subjected himself to many uncomfortable situations and adverse conditions in an attempt to work for God's glory.

Even though he understood the need to suffer himself in order to draw closer to Jesus, St. John was adamantly opposed to treating others with cruelty. As he said, "Who has ever seen people persuaded to love God by harshness?"

St. John the Baptist

Perhaps you've witnessed the wonderful spectacle of an unborn child moving in response to stimuli from the outside world. Well, one saint can claim the honor of responding to the presence of Jesus Christ before he was even born—by kicking while in his mother's womb!

A martyr who was contemporaneous with Jesus and who famously baptized him, St. John the Baptist is considered the forerunner of Jesus. The two men greatly respected and influenced each other, and they shared a common follower base.

As described in the Gospel of John, he was a man sent from God "so that everyone might believe because of his testimony. John himself was not the light; he was simply a witness to tell about the light" (John 1:7–8). In John's own estimation, quoting the words of Isaiah, he was a "voice shouting in the wilderness" (John 1:23).

According to the Gospel of Luke, Elizabeth and Zechariah miraculously conceived John the Baptist. The couple had long since abandoned their hope of having a child due to their advanced age. But one day, while at the temple, Zechariah—a priest in Jerusalem—was visited by the angel Gabriel, who foretold that Elizabeth would become pregnant against all odds.

The angel described Zechariah's future child to him in great detail. The child would be called John, many would celebrate his birth, and he would bring joy to many through his life. Further, John was prophesied to convert many children of Israel to the Lord their God.

What a huge prediction this was! Zechariah was reeling. He had walked into the temple that day expecting the ordinary. What he got was an overwhelming account of a big future involving a child he never expected he would be able to have.

For this reason, Zechariah was doubtful. He expressed his skepticism to the angel, who was displeased. As punishment for his lack of faith, Zechariah was struck mute until the birth of his child.

After Elizabeth became pregnant—as predicted in the angel's proclamation—her friend (and possible cousin) Mary the Blessed Virgin, who was also pregnant, went to see her. As the two women visited, the unborn John the Baptist kicked joyously inside Elizabeth's womb in the presence of Mary and her future child, the Son of God. This memorable incident was John's first act of devotion and exaltation of Jesus in a lifetime that was filled with them.

Once John was born, he indeed fulfilled the specific and critical role that had been predicted for him. Simply put, he prepared the world for Jesus. He traveled extensively for several decades, attracting large crowds who came to hear him preach and be baptized by him.

The beginning and end of John's life serve as vivid bookends to his incredibly important time on Earth. The story of John the Baptist was an eventful one even before he was born; his dramatic death, depicted in Mark 6:14–29, became a popular scene in Christian art.

Like many great Christian martyrs, John the Baptist was killed at the vengeful request of his contemporaries. He "spoke truth to power" to a tetrarch (king's deputy) named Herod, and his candor sparked the jealous rage that brought about John's end.

A bit of background: Herod had divorced his wife, Phasaelis, and taken his brother's wife, Herodias, basically on a romantic whim. John the Baptist spoke out passionately against the immorality of this maneuver. Most leaders do not like to hear words of strong dissent, and given John the Baptist's growing popularity around the Roman Empire, Herod felt extremely threatened by this (just) critique.

On Herod's birthday, his stepdaughter Salome (Herodias's daughter) danced so well for his birthday guests that Herod offered her anything she wanted as a reward. Salome consulted her mother, and Herodias mischievously called for the head of

John the Baptist on a platter. Herod obliged, no doubt gleeful about the "two birds with one stone" benefit of getting to kill his detractor while also delighting his wife, stepdaughter, and their debauched, drunken party guests.

John the Baptist is a rarity among saints, because, according to John 10:41: "John did no miracle." Instead, he proclaimed the truth from the moment he "leapt joyfully" inside his mother's womb in the presence of Jesus, all the way to the moment when he decried Herod for his actions, which cost him his life. For these reasons and others, John the Baptist is a prominent figure in art and literature, and his life serves as a powerful example of courage of conviction and the importance of spiritual support.

St. John the Baptist was the precursor to Jesus, and he had a powerful message that traveled far and wide. As such, he is the patron saint of many far-flung places, including Jordan; Newfoundland and French Canada; Cesena, Florence, Genoa, Monza, and Turin, Italy; Perth, Scotland; Porto, Brazil; and San Juan, Puerto Rico.

John the Baptist is often depicted wearing his animal-skin robe, or bearing a cross, lamb, or scroll with the words *Ecce Agnus Dei* ("Behold the Lamb of God"). As mentioned, the image of the head of St. John the Baptist on a platter is also a popular scene for artists. Sometimes he is seen holding a platter with his own head on it or pouring water from his hands or a scallop shell.

ST. JOSEPH

Did you know that the "Guardian of the Lord" has no recorded words in Scripture? Indeed, St. Joseph—the husband of Mary the Blessed Virgin and the foster father of Jesus Christ—is a bit of an enigma. Both Pope Pius IX and Pope Leo XIII have stated that St. Joseph is the patron and protector of the Catholic Church. But what do we know of this great man's heart and his hopes?

We know Joseph's occupation, but we cannot even be sure of his background or even his age during the events of the New Testament. The Gospels of Luke and Matthew note that he is descended from King David. He was a carpenter, and according to many popular depictions, he may have been elderly. Joseph became betrothed to Mary the Blessed Virgin with the full knowledge and expectation that he would never have relations with his wife, as she had taken a vow of chastity. According to apocryphal writings, he likely had another wife who died and other children.

Joseph was a pious and trusting man, but he was very taken aback to learn of his virgin wife's pregnancy during their betrothal. Upon discovering this shocking development, Joseph adopted a calm and pragmatic approach. He knew that adulterous women were treated harshly in his society, so he resolved to break off his union with Mary gently and quietly send her away.

It's important to note that this response wasn't a show of faithlessness by Joseph. It was simply a demonstration of his devotion to doing the right thing for God and in his society.

What happened to convince him to stay with Mary? The Gospel of Matthew describes four vivid dreams in which Joseph was visited by an angel. The angel predicted, and coached Joseph on, the greatest events of his life and the details of the impending Nativity of Jesus. In the first dream (described in Matthew 1:20–21), the angel assured Joseph that he should continue with his planned marriage to Mary, as she has conceived a child by the Holy Spirit. Joseph took this message to heart.

After the Son of God was born, Joseph experienced his second prophetic dream (Matthew 2:13). In this one, the angel told him to leave Bethlehem (where Jesus had been born) and flee to Egypt because Herod was seeking to murder Jesus. He complied once more.

Once in Egypt, Joseph had his third prophetic dream (Matthew 2:19–20), where the angel told him that it was safe to return to Israel. Again, he heeded the angel's words without question or hesitation.

The fourth and final prophetic dream (Matthew 2:22) is a warning. The angel told Joseph to go to Galilee instead of Judea. True to form, he did as he was told.

What can we learn from St. Joseph's eager obedience to the prophecies of God and of his emissaries? Well, we can clearly see that Joseph was a humble family man with a strong faith.

As far as biblical references go, Joseph is mentioned in Matthew and Luke, and one time in John. There is no reference to Joseph in any of Mark or in the rest of the New Testament. According to popular theory, he died around the time of Jesus's 20th birthday, which explains why Joseph is never mentioned once Jesus begins his public ministry. Therefore, Joseph is, of course, not present for the most momentous occasions of Jesus's adult life—his miracles, his crucifixion, and his resurrection.

Scripture provides scant details about Joseph's personality and his quirks, and instead the Bible focuses on his faith and his strong character. Even still, Joseph is such an admirable, inspiring, and important biblical figure that there is an entire field of study focused on him: Josephology.

As the cornerstone of the family unit for the Son of God, Joseph is no doubt a key figure in Christianity. Joseph has two feast days, March 19 and May 1, to commemorate each of his most important roles—as husband of Mary and as a worker and provider for his family.

In art, St. Joseph is often portrayed as an older man. He's sometimes shown with his staff topped with flowers, a carpenter's square or tools, the infant Jesus in his arms, two turtle doves, or a spikenard flower.

He is the patron saint of the Catholic Church, unborn children, fathers, families, expectant mothers, immigrants, travelers, carpenters, Realtors, employment and working people in general, and happy death (since he was said to have died in the presence of his entire nuclear family, Mary and Jesus). He is also the patron saint of many places, including Canada, Croatia, Korea, and Vietnam, along with Zapotlán, Mexico, and Mandaue City and Cebu, the Philippines.

Have you ever been to a town called San José? Any town bearing that name is paying tribute to St. Joseph, and it's in good company—San José is the most common place name in the world!

Indeed, the simple power of Joseph's story has inspired people all over the world. He is one of the most popular saints, and it's not hard to see why. What is known of his life is filled with such selfless and inspiring acts. It is thanks to Joseph's calm, steady presence that Mary the Blessed Virgin was cared for, loved, and protected in the most sensitive time of her life, as she nurtured Jesus Christ.

For a man who is given no quotations in the Bible, Joseph's story is strong proof of the old saying that actions speak louder than words!

St. Jude

Shakespeare wrote: "What's in a name? That which we call a rose by any other name would smell as sweet." But this isn't strictly true where saints are involved—names are very important! For evidence of this, just look at the case of St. Jude, a Christ-loving martyr of the 1st century A.D. who shares a name with the biggest turncoat in the Bible.

When we hear "Judas" and "disciple," our minds immediately light on betrayal. Judas Iscariot is infamous for double-crossing Jesus, leading him to his arrest, trial, and crucifixion. But what about the other Jude? St. Jude was also one of the 12 apostles of Jesus. Although his full name was Judas Thaddeus, he was some-times known instead as Thaddeus, Jude of James, or Lebbaeus.

St. Jude's reputation is quite different from Judas Iscariot's, of course. St. Jude was present at the Last Supper, and he is remem-bered for asking Jesus why he would not make himself known to the world following his resurrection.

A preacher in Judea, Samaria, Idumaea, Syria, Mesopotamia, and Libya, Jude wrote an epistle to the Churches of the East, in which he spoke out against the heresies of the Simonians, the Nicolaites, and the Gnostics. According to scholars, Jude's mother, Mary, was cousin to Mary the Blessed Virgin. Jude returned to Jerusalem in A.D. 62 to help elect his brother St. Simeon as Bishop of Jerusalem. Jude was likely a farmer.

Beyond these basic facts, Jude's biographical information is uncertain at best. He may have been a vegetarian, and he may have had a father named Clopas who was martyred due to his devotion to Christ. Jude may have been the brother of St. James the Less, also one of the apostles. St. Jude and St. James the Less were possibly the cousins of Jesus.

St. Jude was martyred along with Simon the Zealot around A.D. 65, although accounts vary as to whether it was in Beirut or

Persia. There are also different tales as to the manner of his death; some say he was hacked to death with an ax, others that he was beaten with a club before his dead body was beheaded with an ax. This is why St. Jude is commonly depicted in art with either a club or an ax.

St. Jude's body was brought to Rome following his martyrdom. He was placed in a crypt in St. Peter's Basilica, and the site quickly became an important place of pilgrimage.

According to popular account, many pilgrims who visited there experienced powerful miracles. For this reason, Jude's reputation as patron saint of "the hopeless and despaired" was established. Further, both St. Bridget of Sweden and St. Bernard had visions from God in which he requested that they recognize St. Jude as the "patron saint of the impossible."

Despite his sketchy biography, St. Jude has exhibited the power to inspire many people over many centuries. Along with the apostle Bartholomew, St. Jude is credited with having brought Christianity to Armenia. (Both are recognized as the patron saints of the Armenian Apostolic Church.)

St. Judas Thaddeus gained his reputation as "patron saint of lost causes" in part due to his commonly being confused with Judas Iscariot. Many Christians hesitated to say St. Jude's name for fear of inadvertently calling Christ's betrayer! According to this idea, the eager St. Jude became so unused to hearing his name invoked that he went above and beyond to help anyone who called to him—even in the most desperate circumstances. He is also credited with helping people heal by reminding them of the power and passion of God's Word.

St. Jude is the patron saint of many places, including Armenia; St. Petersburg, Florida; Lucena, Quezon, Sibalom, and Trece Mártires, the Philippines; and Sinajana, Guam. He is the patron saint of the Chicago Police Department and the Clube de Regatas do

Flamengo in Rio de Janeiro, Brazil. Famously, he is the namesake for St. Jude's Children's Research Hospital.

St. Jude is often depicted with a club, ax, boat, oar, or medallion and with a flame above his head, in reference to his presence at the Pentecost, where he and the other apostles received the Holy Spirit. Many times, he is shown carrying a small image of Jesus, in reference to one of his miracles as a proselytizer. King Abagar of Edessa wrote to ask Jesus to cure his leprosy, and he dispatched an artist to deliver the letter and bring back a drawing of Jesus. Jesus rubbed his face on a cloth, leaving his image behind, and passed it on to St. Jude, who presented it to King Abagar, who was then cured.

St. Kateri Tekakwitha

The first Native American saint, Kateri Tekakwitha lived a pious and inspiring life within the conflict-ridden environment of 17th-century North America.

A Christian convert, Kateri observed many of the austere customs favored by monks, nuns, and others who have strived to live a life in imitation of Christ. For example, she pursued voluntary suffering, meditation, and charity. She took a chastity vow, even though there was no precedent for women of her community to remain unmarried in adulthood.

Indeed, among the canon of the saints, there is one key, impressive distinction about Kateri. Owing to the isolation of her community and the justifiable suspicion they harbored toward outsiders, Kateri was not directly taught many of the traditional Christian practices she adopted. She simply took them on out of a purity of spirit and a gentleness of heart. She led an extremely Christian life by "instinct"—or by divine guidance.

Born to a Christian Algonquin mother and a Mohawk chief, Kateri was orphaned at only four years old, when a smallpox epidemic claimed her parents and brother. Kateri herself was left with massive scarring and severe vision loss from the disease. She was adopted by her uncle, who became the new Mohawk chief following her father's death.

Her uncle intensely distrusted the "black robes"—as the Jesuit missionaries were called—and his dislike and distaste for Christianity proved to be a challenge as young Kateri grew more interested in her faith. This was one of the many conditions that limited Kateri's formal exposure to Christian practices.

All Kateri ever knew was the proud, strong tradition of her Iroquois and Mohawk ancestors, which dictated a life filled with hard work, marriage, and belief in the spirit-based religion of her tribes. And indeed, Kateri thrived as a young adolescent in her society.

She became highly skilled at traditional tribal pastimes, such as making clothes from animal pelts, weaving mats and baskets from grasses, gathering fruits, and preparing game.

But even while recognizing the richness of her background, Kateri could not resist her growing affinity for Christianity. At first, she tiptoed toward conversion with small acts of rebellion, such as refusing to entertain any of the suitors her family had arranged for her.

By 19, Kateri made the brave and definitive step of becoming baptized. She took the name Kateri, after St. Catherine of Siena. She stunned her family and community by announcing that she would never marry—just like her namesake, Kateri would be "the bride of Jesus Christ"—and she would not work on Sunday.

There was great local opposition to Kateri's religious awakening. Her conversion became so polarizing that she knew she had to flee for her own safety. She stole away in the dead of night on the advice of a priest and made a 200-mile journey on foot to a Native American Christian village in Canada.

For Kateri, her new Canadian home was like a refuge. She nurtured her faith among the safety of a loving and like-minded community. It was in these years, spanning the time when Kateri was about 20 to 23 years old, that the young woman lived a nearly monastic life.

She sought nothing more than to deprive herself of all comforts—an incredibly bold and unusual impulse in an era already so filled with pain and hardship. Kateri was so moved by a love of God that she fasted regularly and participated in mortification of the flesh (usually by placing thorns in her bed). When Kateri did eat, she often added unappetizing ingredients to her food so that consuming it would not be pleasurable.

What incredible discipline! Even as St. Kateri suffered the mental strain and social anguish of religious persecution, she still pursued the physical discomforts of fasting and penances. The fire of Christ burned inside Kateri, and it's hard not to be inspired by her passionate example.

Unfortunately, her regular penances and fasts put her in somewhat weak health, and around Easter of 1680, St. Kateri died, at the age of 24.

On her death, miraculously, the smallpox scars that had disfigured Kateri's face disappeared completely, leaving her with smooth skin and a radiant smile.

Have you ever felt like Kateri, condemned because of your beliefs? Perhaps you were thrust into a situation where you didn't feel that you fit in. Sometimes, life places us in "transitional" moments, where we are called to make positive contributions to, and to gain valuable personal insights from, an environment or situation that doesn't feel comfortable. Sometimes these uncomfortable moments are the perfect incubator for the discoveries or breakthroughs that we need!

St. Kateri was intimately familiar with suffering—both from the rampant hardships and diseases of her time, and from the ascetic lifestyle she so eagerly pursued. St. Kateri exuded that highly Christian quality of contentment through complete submission.

She is the patron saint of ecology, the environment, people in exile, people who have lost their parents, people ridiculed for their piety, and Native Americans. The "Lily of the Mohawks" is often depicted with her signature lily, turtle, and rosary. Her simple life of unwavering devotion to her faith, in a rugged and remote time and place, serves as a powerful reminder that God is *everywhere*.

ST. MARIA GORETTI

The best stories are about ordinary people acting with extraordinary courage. This is especially true of St. Maria Goretti, a poor Italian girl who lived a tragically short life and suffered a brutal death. While the details of her story are gruesome, it's impossible not to be inspired by Maria's maturity, compassion, and forgiveness.

Born to impoverished tenant farmers in rural Italy, Maria lost her father when she was nine years old. With this loss of the family breadwinner, the Gorettis had to adjust—Maria and her siblings began working in the fields to earn money, and the family had to move in with another local family, the Serenellis, to save money. This desperate move set off the chain of events that led to Maria's death—but also to her eventual canonization.

As Maria sat outside mending a shirt one day, the rowdy teenager Alessandro Serenelli made sexual advances toward her. Maria was about 11 at the time, and Alessandro was around 18. Maria valiantly refused.

Even through her fear and exhaustion, Maria appealed to Alessandro to stop. She was outmatched in size, but the power of her faith was undeniable. As he lunged at her, she screamed: "God does not want it! You will go to hell!" An immense physical struggle ensued, and Maria told Alessandro she would rather die than submit to him.

This only made Alessandro more enraged, and he stabbed Maria 14 times. She was taken to the hospital and underwent surgery without anesthesia, but her life could not be saved. She passed away, telling her doctor she would pray for him, and emphasizing that she forgave her attacker. Maria even went so far as to state that she hoped to see Alessandro in heaven with her!

Alessandro was tried and imprisoned for his crime—he spent the next 27 years in jail. He avoided being executed because he was tried as a minor, and also because Maria's mother had testified at his trial, requesting mercy.

Prison proved to be a highly beneficial place for Alessandro. He used the time to pray and reflect on his actions. One day, he had a vision of Maria visiting him and offering him lilies. But when he reached for them, they burned in his hands.

Upon being released, Alessandro went straight to Maria's mother to beg for her forgiveness. Maria's mother granted it, noting, "If Maria forgave you, I can too."

Alessandro spent the rest of his life trying to make up for the grave error of his youth. Eventually, he became a laybrother of the Order of Friars Minor Capuchin. He lived in the monastery and worked as its receptionist and gardener until his death at age 87. While the details of his attack were appalling, the penitence he showed for the next seven decades of his life is inspiring.

On a pleasant day in June 1950, Maria was canonized in a ceremony in the Piazza San Pietro outside St. Peter's Basilica. Calling her "St. Agnes of the 20th Century," Pius XII led the praises for the strong and faithful young girl whose short life had inspired so many.

And indeed, many people were inspired to pay tribute to her story. St. Maria Goretti's canonization drew one of the largest crowds in history, with a gathering of about half a million!

Several miracles involving her family members are attributed to St. Maria. According to her brother Angelo, Maria appeared to him in a vision to tell him to immigrate to America. This move proved extremely profitable and helpful in his life. Independently, Maria's brother Mariano claimed to have experienced a vision of Maria while fighting in the trenches as a soldier in World War I. Maria told him to stay in the trenches while the rest of his unit charged the Germans; Mariano was the sole survivor of his unit.

St. Maria wanted nothing more than to forgive and to love. She is often depicted wearing simple peasant clothing and holding a knife or 14 lilies. She is the patron saint of young people, especially girls.

It's not always easy to follow the example of divine forgiveness. Yet St. Maria Goretti shows us through her graceful example that life can be so meaningful and rewarding when we choose to use our light to love and inspire others—not to dwell in the darkness.

ST. MARY MAGDALENE

Have you ever dyed an Easter egg? If the answer is yes, then you were paying tribute to Mary Magdalene!

The so-called apostle of apostles, Mary was a contemporary of Jesus who played a key role in discovering and spreading the word of his resurrection. According to popular tradition, she "invented" the dyed Easter egg. In fact, it was a visual cue she used to demonstrate the power and beauty of Christ's sacrifice.

A friend and confidante to Jesus, St. Mary Magdalene is one of the most well-known and frequently referenced figures from the Bible. She washed Jesus's feet and appeared at the tomb after his crucifixion. She is often depicted in art and popular culture—from classical paintings to the modern bestseller and blockbuster film *The Da Vinci Code*.

There are inconsistencies and contradictions among all these portrayals. The confusion is further compounded by the fact that "Mary" is such a common name in the era of the New Testament. There is the Virgin Mary, Mary of Bethany (sister of Martha and Lazarus), and Mary Magdalene. There are also satellite figures—Mary, the mother of James, and Mary Salome, for example—which add to the puzzle.

But many people, when they hear "Mary Magdalene," have a clear mental image of her washing Jesus's feet and drying them, her long hair spilling over her bare shoulder, from Luke 7:36–50.

She is a complex figure in biblical narratives and has been invoked throughout history to serve as a banner-bearer for various causes. Indeed, she has been turned into a representative for feminism and for fallen women alike! Some hold her out as a former "loose woman" and repentant sinner, others as the steadfast model of lifelong religiosity. Whatever the associations we've attached to her name, though, she was a tenderhearted caregiver. She was also a devoted follower of Jesus during his time of public ministry. And during his persecution, her role became even more memorable. It was St. Mary Magdalene who saw firsthand Jesus's crucifixion, his burial, and his resurrection.

In John 20:1, St. Mary Magdalene traveled to Jesus's tomb and discovered it to be empty. Mark 16:9, Matthew 28:1, and Luke 24:10 each provide varying accounts of the characters who accompanied her at this critical moment, but the important part is Mary's presence, which is indisputable.

In his 1988 apostolic letter titled "On the Dignity and Vocation of Women," Pope John Paul II wrote: "Mary Magdalene was the first eyewitness of the Risen Christ, and for this reason she was also the first to bear witness to him before the Apostles."

Think of a time when you were called to "spread the good news" about something. When we are the first to discover a secret, it's only natural to sometimes feel a mix of pride and dread. What a great honor Mary Magdalene received when she viewed Jesus's resurrection. On the other hand, it's always a burden to try to convince doubtful people of a miraculous event!

One way that Mary handled this responsibility was with her Easter eggs. According to tradition, she attended a lavish royal banquet at the estate of the Roman emperor Tiberius. This dinner happened shortly after the death and resurrection of Jesus, when curiosity about the wondrous event was at a fever pitch. Bursting with excitement for Christ, Mary Magdalene greeted the arrogant and secular emperor by announcing, "Christ is risen!"

Tiberius laughed in her face, retorting that the idea that Christ had risen from the dead was just as ridiculous as saying that the egg Mary Magdalene held in her hand would turn red. Before Tiberius had finished his sentence, the egg did just that!

St. Mary Magdalene is the patron saint of people who are ridiculed for their piety, apothecaries, people struggling with sexual temptation, perfumeries, pharmacists, tanners, those trying to live a contemplative life, and Altrani and Casamicciola Terme in Italy.

If you have ever experienced the sensation of having to convince those around you of something impossible sounding, then St. Mary Magdalene is a wonderful saint to draw inspiration from! Regardless of the specific details of her life, she was a key member of Jesus's support system. She loved to be near him and to praise and spread his teachings. And he was certainly strengthened and steadied by her constant presence.

On Mount Athos in Greece, the holy relic of St. Mary Magdalene is kept inside the Simonopetra Monastery. Pilgrims who visited this sacred treasure have reported that it is incorrupt, and that the preserved hand smells of heavenly flowers.

St. Mary Magdalene is often depicted in art with an alabaster box of ointment, a container filled with myrrh, and the Easter egg that she powerfully turned red in Emperor Tiberius's presence. She is often depicted embracing the feet of Christ, and this vivid and humble pose is a wonderful demonstration of her quiet passion and unwavering devotion.

ST. MARY
THE BLESSED VIRGIN

St. Mary the Blessed Virgin has perhaps the most nicknames of all the saints. There are the honorific ones: Blessed Virgin Mary, Mother of God, Our Lady (*Madonna*, in medieval Italian), and Queen of Heaven. In antiquity, she was also known as "God-bearer," "Ever-virgin," and "All-holy" to the Greeks.

For Catholics, St. Mary the Blessed Virgin is the greatest and holiest among all saints. As such, she has many names! St. Mary is most widely known by such descriptors as Our Lady of Sorrows, Our Lady of Good Counsel, Our Lady of Navigators, and even Our Lady Undoer of Knots.

This huge array of distinctive and superlative nicknames underscores St. Mary's importance. The simple act of hearing her name can be powerful enough to remind people all around the world, and all across the ages, of the humble faith and maternal love that informs all the greatest parts of humanity. As mentioned earlier, the term *hyperdulia* is used to describe the particular veneration of Mary by her most devout followers.

Mary was born in Jerusalem, and she took a vow of virginity early. One day while living in Nazareth, Mary experienced a vision of the archangel Gabriel. He told her a huge piece of news: She was to become the mother of Jesus, and her child would be conceived through the Holy Spirit!

Mary was shaken, but she continued about her everyday life while considering the import of this message. She said, almost with resignation: "I am the Lord's servant. May everything you have said about me come true" (Luke 1:38).

Consider how much restraint and faith this required. It takes a great amount of resolve to accept your future, especially when that future involves such a massive, world-changing responsibility!

As a sworn virgin, Mary carefully chose for herself a future husband who would help her uphold her vow. She sought a man who would watch over and support her and found that in St. Joseph.

During her betrothal to Joseph, Mary became pregnant with the Son of God, as prophesied by Gabriel. At first, Joseph was alarmed—he did not want to cause a scene, but he made firm plans to break up with Mary quietly and send her away in order to spare her the shame and public ridicule that came with adultery. But after Mary explained the divine origins of her pregnancy, Joseph lent her the protection and support that she most needed. Together, of course, they traveled to Bethlehem for the census, and Mary gave birth to Jesus.

Those are the widely cited facts of St. Mary's life. We all know instinctively that she was a truly wonderful mother to the Son of God—she nurtured him in body, as well as mind and spirit. But what are the less-known details of the Blessed Virgin's life? How did she support her beloved son and move him toward changing the world, and the course of humanity?

Jesus's first recorded miracle occurred when he turned water into wine at a wedding at Cana. It was St. Mary who alerted her son to the fact that the wine had run out. She prodded him to take action and instructed the servants at the wedding to do whatever her son told them.

What a perfect example of parental encouragement! We may see elements of ourselves in this anecdote—who can't relate to the moment when a parent pushes a doubting child to live up to their potential? Anyone might feel reluctance and sheepishness—even Jesus! He first responded to his mother: "Dear woman, that's not our problem . . . My time has not yet come" (John 2:4). Sometimes, only a mother can see when we are ready to share our light with the world!

St. Mary carried and gave birth to the Savior of humanity, so naturally she is the patroness of all humanity. Generally speaking, she is the patron saint of any good or worthwhile endeavor.

St. Maximilian Kolbe

When was the last time you found yourself at a crossroads? In our everyday lives, we are often called to make a choice between two mutually exclusive options.

How do you feel in these moments? Do you press forward boldly, secure in your decision? Or do you hesitate and delay, always wondering later whether you made the right choice? And when your two options are either "safe and comfortable" or "difficult and dangerous," which of these do you most often choose?

St. Maximilian Kolbe was a Polish Franciscan friar who lived through an incredibly challenging historical era—the Holocaust in German-occupied Poland—but who constantly made incredibly brave and inspiring choices. He continually took the "difficult and dangerous" option, beginning from when he first felt called to lead a religious life.

In 1906, when Maximilian Kolbe was only 12 years old, he experienced a powerful vision of the Virgin Mary. As he described it:

> The Mother of God came to me holding two crowns—one white, the other red. She asked me if I was willing to accept either. The white one meant that I should persevere in purity, and the red that I should become a martyr. I said I would accept them both.

What courageous poise! Obviously, Maximilian came of age in a treacherous time. The political instability leading up to World War II certainly forced many European children to grow up fast. But Maximilian's early devotion to Mary was admirable.

Even as the world around him was turned upside down, he enjoyed the consistent comforts of praying to the Blessed

Virgin—who never deserts us, even when our situation at first appears to be bleak.

The following year, Maximilian and his brother Francis joined the Conventual Franciscan minor seminary. By the time Maximilian took his final vows seven years later, in 1914, he had adopted the additional name of Maria—a fitting tribute to the saint who set him on the path of God to begin with.

After the seminary, Maximilian earned doctorates in philosophy and theology in Rome. Throughout his scholarship and his travels, he continued to devote himself to consecrating Mary and entrusting himself to her. But the university environment exposed Maximilian to a faction of dissenters he had never encountered before. During a Freemason anniversary celebration, Maximilian witnessed a violent protest against Pope St. Pius X and Pope Benedict XV. Afterward, he created the monthly devotional periodical called *Rycerz Niepokalanej* (Knight of the Immaculate) while working as a priest.

During the 1930s, Maximilian turned to missionary work, traveling to China, Japan, and India. In Japan, he founded a monastery that remains to this day, nestled among the traditional Shinto temples of the area. He returned to Poland in 1936 due to failing health stemming from complications of tuberculosis.

By 1940, Polish citizens faced problems like food and commodity shortages, currency instability, and terrible ethnic persecution. Many fled the country, but Maximilian stayed—he knew his help at home was needed now more than ever.

As time passed, conditions only grew more tense. Maximilian, who was ethnically German from his father's side, was presented with the opportunity to sign the *Deutsche Volksliste*, a declaration that would afford him certain protections reserved for German people.

He refused—Maximilian knew that such an action would seem to validate the idea that non-German people should be treated differently. In refusing to sign and thus placing himself in danger, Maximilian demonstrated yet another selfless act in a lifetime filled with them.

Eventually, Maximilian was called to suffer even further, when he was taken to the prison camp at Auschwitz in May 1941. Even among the deplorable conditions there, Maximilian served as a beacon of hope for his fellow man by acting as a priest.

A few months later, Maximilian adopted the formal red martyr crown that his beloved St. Mary had presented to him as a child. When a camp commander selected Maximilian's cellmate to be starved to death in an underground bunker, Maximilian volunteered to take his place.

In two weeks with no food, Maximilian led his fellow prisoners in prayer to Our Lady. By the end of the second week, only Maximilian remained alive, and he was in peaceful spirits. Frustrated, the guards decided to give him a lethal injection of carbolic acid—and St. Maximilian raised his arm calmly to receive it.

His beatification miracles included curing a case of intestinal tuberculosis in 1948 and a case of arterial sclerosis in 1950.

St. Maximilian is the patron saint of families, incarcerated people, journalists, political prisoners, amateur radio enthusiasts, and the pro-life movement.

Although our choices may not be as high-stakes or as bold as St. Maximilian's, we are called to make powerful and consequential decisions every day of our lives. Doing so may not feel comfortable or easy. But if we hold God in our hearts and show love and kindness to our neighbors, we can be certain that we are making the right moves!

If you are unsure or wavering, take heart by looking to Maximilian's example and his beautiful life of committed action.

ST. MOTHER TERESA

There's nothing like the excitement of a new project! Each time you embark on a different path, you are writing a new chapter in your own autobiography. You feel excitement—anticipation for what's to come—mixed with a bit of natural anxiety, of course, along with eagerness to make a positive impact.

For St. Teresa of Calcutta, also known as Mother Teresa, a new chapter of her religious life turned out to be something even greater and more meaningful than she ever could have dreamed.

Born to Albanian parents in present-day Macedonia, Gonxha Bojaxhiu lived a calm and comfortable early life. All that changed when her father, the owner of a successful construction business, died suddenly.

As Gonxha learned about Catholicism in school, she felt the pull of missionary work abroad. So upon turning 18, she joined the Loreto Sisters of Dublin. A year later, she was sent to the Loreto novitiate in Darjeeling, India—a move that would forever change her life. It was there that she adopted the name Teresa, after St. Thérèse of Lisieux.

In India, Teresa took a job teaching history and geography at a private school for the wealthy of Calcutta. But she began to feel bothered by the gulf between the way her well-to-do students lived and the practical realities of slum life around the city.

When she was 36 years old, the woman who would become known to the world as Mother Teresa had an epiphany. As she rode the train to Darjeeling, she heard "a call within a call." She realized she could make a greater impact by venturing out of the convent and fostering an intimate and meaningful connection to India's poor among the slums.

Teresa lost no time after receiving her call. She secured permission to leave her convent and become a missionary. To accomplish her ultimate goal of opening a new religious order, she knew she would need more resources and skills. She took a crash course in nursing, then headed back to Calcutta, where she opened a school for the poor and adopted a daily uniform of simple white sari and sandals. She wanted to get her hands dirty, so to speak.

The simple power of Mother Teresa's ministry spread quickly. Her idea—of experiencing firsthand the hardships of the slums—seemed radical at first. But people soon realized that there could be no greater way to connect with and understand this population but to live among them.

Her work inched forward at first, as Mother Teresa fought the usual obstacles of lack of recognition, low funds, and institutional resistance. Slowly but surely, she built more and more missions, care facilities, and refuge centers. As news of her service traveled around the world, thanks in large part to the mass media of modern times, Mother Teresa received the benefit of donations in the form of food, clothes, medicine, and even buildings.

As the resources grew, the scope of her work expanded as well. Mother Teresa set out on her path because she wanted to address the unique and specific problems that come from overcrowding and limited resources. She had a vision to live among the poorest of the poor in the slums.

But soon, Mother Teresa's ministry to the poor expanded its reach. Through her facilities, she began to offer services to orphans, abandoned children, alcoholics, and the aging. Her work was devoted to identifying and assisting those who struggled most, whether physically, emotionally, or societally. Her work garnered global accolades—she received the Nobel Peace Prize in 1979.

By the time of her death in 1996, Mother Teresa had opened 517 missions in over 100 countries. Speaking of her uniquely modern global approach, she said: "By blood, I am Albanian. By citizenship, an Indian. By faith, I am a Catholic nun. As to my calling, I belong to the world. As to my heart, I belong entirely to the Heart of Jesus."

Could Teresa have imagined that her work would take on such a life of its own as she sat on that train to Darjeeling so many decades earlier?

Have you ever experienced a moment of this kind of clarity? How did you handle it? Often, the most meaningful moments of our lives—the times at which we have epiphanies and make choices that define us forever—arise under unassuming, everyday circumstances. Take comfort in the natural flow of your goodness!

Teresa of Calcutta was canonized in September of 2016, after her official miracles were widely reported and rigorously vetted. She is credited with healing an abdominal tumor in 2002, and the cure of a deadly bacterial brain infection in 2008.

Nobody knows your struggle more than St. Teresa of Calcutta, who willingly chose to live among the poorest of the poor in order to better serve them.

ST. NICHOLAS

It's hard not to feel cheered when we hear the name "St. Nicholas." Besides Mary the Blessed Virgin, he is considered to be the saint most widely depicted in art. This is, of course, due to the fact that his name is synonymous with Santa Claus. Who doesn't smile and laugh (and get excited about presents) upon thinking of the good-natured, rotund St. Nick?

Before he got his close modern association with gift giving and Christmas, St. Nicholas was a 4th-century Greek bishop in Asia Minor. An only child, Nicholas was quite religious from an early age, even to the point where he observed canonical fasts twice weekly during his youth.

Young Nicholas became an orphan when his well-to-do parents died unexpectedly during an epidemic. Nicholas was raised by an uncle, who was also a bishop.

Sometimes, life takes unexpected turns. This was the case with Nicholas. When he went to live with his uncle, he gained a firsthand look at the power and purpose of religion. Nicholas's uncle stoked in his nephew the fires of his spiritual passion, teaching him about his own profession and experiences. Thanks in part to that, Nicholas became a bishop at a young age.

He impressed many with his zeal and piety, and with an early knack for performing miracles. In one case, famine and food shortages gripped his hometown. A devious butcher caught and killed three young children, planning to sell them as ham. Nicholas condemned the horrible butcher and resurrected the children through his prayers.

In another miraculous instance—also during a famine—a ship loaded with wheat was anchored in a nearby harbor, as the sailors prepared to bring it to Constantinople. Nicholas boarded the ship and requested a small amount of wheat in order to help his starving community. The sailors refused—they did not want to get in trouble in Constantinople if their freight was light.

Nicholas promised this would not be a problem. The sailors gave him an amount of wheat to feed the famished, and sure enough, when the ship reached Constantinople, the volume of wheat was miraculously replenished!

But the miracle that St. Nicholas is most known for involves a spectacular moment of charity. Nicholas encountered a man who who could not afford dowries for his three daughters. Without intervention, the daughters would remain unmarried and might even have faced a life of prostitution in order to make money.

Though Nicholas was moved by this father's plight, he did not want to call attention to himself or embarrass the man. So he went to visit the poor man's house in the middle of the night and threw three purses filled with gold coins—one for each daughter—through a window.

According to the traditional story of St. Nicholas, the father tried hard to determine the identity of his benefactor. But again, Nicholas was most concerned with helping others, not with bringing glory to himself. And so he took great pains to conceal his identity, telling the man that he should focus on God's love instead. Even so great a man as St. Nicholas thought of himself merely as God's errand runner. What a powerful and humbling message!

Have you ever participated in a "Secret Santa" pool? Now you know the saintly origins of this fun and wonderful tradition.

And if you find yourself being in a time of need like the penniless man with the three daughters, remind yourself that God's helpers are always right around the corner. You can promote selfless acts of "Secret Santa" giving—or be the beneficiary of them—at any time of the year! Think of this lesson about the beauty of helping others anonymously, and take heart.

St. Nicholas is the patron saint of all these gift-giving parties, as well as of repentant thieves, brewers, pharmacists, archers, and pawnbrokers. He is considered the patron and protector of Aberdeen, Scotland; Galway, Ireland; Liverpool, England; Moscow, Russia; Bari, Italy; Amsterdam, the Netherlands; Lorraine, France; and all of Greece.

You may have a mental image of St. Nicholas as a cuddly, chubby old man. This depiction seems mostly historically consistent—with the exception of the overweight part! St. Nicholas lived in a time of shortage and famine, and he surely would have prioritized the feeding of others over his own comforts.

In art, St. Nicholas is often shown in his bishop garb, with Jesus Christ looking over one shoulder, and is frequently depicted wearing an omophorion vestment or carrying a Gospel book. In life and legend, "Jolly Old St. Nick" loved nothing better than to give and promote good.

St. Padre Pio

Pray, hope, and don't worry. This was a mantra of St. Padre Pio—what simple but beautiful advice! Though he lived for eight decades, Padre Pio was afflicted with asthmatic bronchitis, kidney stones, abdominal pain and inflammation, and ulcers throughout his life. It is safe to assume that his body was in pain more often than not, but his mind and his spirituality only grew stronger with each trial.

Think of a time when you felt tremendous distress. Did you pray, hope, and stop yourself from worrying? It's not always easy to surrender to God's plan. In fact, "giving up" our feelings of control can be one of the scariest things that we do. Thankfully, trusting in your faith is often the most foolproof way to end your anxiety.

A Capuchin friar, St. Padre Pio was born Francesco Forgione in 19th-century Italy. In his 81 years of life, St. Padre Pio spread the word of God through his work as a priest and mystic, and through the publicity he received as a person who experienced stigmata.

His family was not rich by any means, but they were highly religious. In his hometown of Pietrelcina, Francesco and his family attended Mass every day and prayed the Rosary every night.

Even within Francesco's deeply religious home community, the young saint was particularly spiritual. As a child, he frequently saw visions of Jesus, the Virgin Mary, and his guardian angel. Francesco communicated with them frequently, and they became so familiar to him that he didn't realize that his peers weren't seeing the same things he was.

Padre Pio experienced a lifetime of physical suffering. At six, he suffered his first major bout with illness, after he contracted a near-deadly case of gastroenteritis. Several years later, he caught typhoid fever. At age 17, Fra Pio (as he was then known, having taken the Franciscan habit) fell terribly ill again. During his seven-year academic course to become a priest, Fra Pio suffered from horrible symptoms like fainting, migraines, fatigue, and chronic nausea. He subsisted on a diet of milk and cheese, since those were the only foods that he could keep down. In the early years, Fra Pio was weak and frail. He struggled to complete the rigorous activities required for his training and education.

But it was in this time of acute physical distress that Fra Pio drew even closer to God. He prayed constantly—not only for relief of his pain, but for guidance and direction on his path. He was in constant communication with God, Jesus, Mary, and his guardian angel. In fact, one of the friars studying with Pio at the time reported seeing him levitating above the ground, in total ecstasy as he conversed with his cherished spiritual beings.

What an inspiration! Imagine being so confident in God's plan that the tougher your challenges, the closer you grew to him. It's only natural to feel very human emotions like uncertainty, confusion, and even frustration when times are hard. But what if you considered your moments of greatest difficulty as spiritual bonding opportunities rather than setbacks?

Padre Pio's absolute trust in the Creator continued even as his health declined. At 31 years old, Padre Pio experienced his first bout of the stigmata. As he heard confessions, Padre Pio's skin began to bleed, bruise, and ache with absolutely no physical cause. Soon it became clear to Padre Pio that the wounds corresponded exactly to the crucifixion marks of Jesus. After this first incident, the stigmata episodes continued for the rest of his life—another 50 years!

Each time Padre Pio experienced the stigmata, onlookers noticed that the bleeding wounds smelled sweet and floral, and they never became infected. Doctors, including even skeptical medical experts, examined the marks and were unable to find a reasonable explanation.

Even as Padre Pio was beginning to emerge as a spiritual authority, he also offered inspiration to Italians who had suffered economic ruin after the first World War. His many unexplained gifts—from his visions to his levitations, to even more fantastical abilities such as bilocation, prophecy, and sustaining long periods without food or rest—served as a beacon of hope during a very dark period.

During a series of official inquiries both before and after his death, the legitimacy of St. Padre Pio's talents and abilities was reasonably affirmed. By 1999, Padre Pio was beatified, and Pope John Paul II canonized him in 2002.

The simplicity of Padre Pio's teachings holds universal appeal. True to his Franciscan roots, he emphasized the beauty of nature, the dangers of materialism, and the joys of giving. Those lessons remain just as fresh in the present day, of course! Padre Pio always stressed that true enlightenment comes from seeking to know God, affirming your faith daily, and striving for constant self-improvement.

Padre Pio is the patron saint of civil defense volunteers, teens, people who feel stressed, and people who experience seasonal affective disorder. He is also the patron saint of Italy and Malta.

A lifelong healer and helper, St. Padre Pio compiled a list of recognized miracles involving incredible cases of healing and recovery, including tumors and chronic inflammations. In life, he helped many who suffered physical or emotional trauma; after his death in 1968, even more miraculous cures have been credited to him.

If you're looking for more general guidance, St. Padre Pio offers a powerful reminder that attitude is everything. He was never known to complain about his many ailments, and when he found himself receiving more publicity thanks to his God-given gifts, he never sought to abuse his platform or enrich himself personally from the attention. God handed him ups and downs during his long life, but through it all, St. Padre Pio kept praying and never worried.

ST. PATRICK

When you experience an uncomfortable event, it's normal to develop an aversion for the conditions that brought you there and avoid revisiting them. But St. Patrick, the patron saint of Ireland, did just the opposite.

Born to a well-to-do family in 5th-century Britain, Patrick got quite the shock to the system when he was captured by Irish pirates while sitting at home one day. He was only 16 years old!

As Patrick described in his writing *The Confession*, his captivity in Ireland was life-changing. Patrick's captors forced him to work as a shepherd, and he used the long silences of that job to reflect and grow spiritually. Reflecting on his stint as a prisoner in Ireland, St. Patrick thought that God had shown mercy on his youth and ignorance and had given him a way—however roundabout— to reconsider his priorities.

The next phase of Patrick's life taught him the value of trusting God. After six years as an enslaved shepherd in Ireland, a voice told him that he would be returning home soon, and that he would travel by sea.

Hearing this assurance gave Patrick the confidence to flee from his captors, so one night he traveled some 200 miles to a faraway port where he knew nobody. He talked his way onto a boat, and after a three-day sailing journey, he found himself back on the shores of Britain.

Once Patrick made it back to his home country, he still had a long way to go. The ship he had come in on was out of supplies and had gotten sidetracked from its original destination. So Patrick (along with the rest of the people on board) were left to forage and wander for 28 days in a remote area. Soon, everyone was becoming faint and delirious with hunger.

But Patrick kept a sharp mind, and the incident provided a wonderful opportunity to test out the maturity and patience that he had learned from his conversations with God. St. Patrick urged his shipmates to join him in a prayer for food, and because they were so desperate, everyone went along with this. Shortly after, the whole group came upon a herd of wild boar—a miraculous occurrence that gave them the confidence (and calories!) to keep going.

Several years later, after Patrick had readjusted to life back home in Britain, he found himself experiencing powerful flashbacks of his Irish captivity. He started having visions of a man named Victorious, who carried a bunch of letters in his arms.

In this vision, Victorious handed Patrick a letter, which said THE VOICE OF THE IRISH on top. As Patrick began to read the letter, he started hearing a crowd of voices. They said in unison: "We appeal to you, holy servant boy, to come and walk among us."

Wow. Have you ever experienced a dream or a vision that was so vivid? And it's not just the details that made it so for Patrick, of course—it was a vivid vision because it told him exactly who needed his help, and what he needed to do!

Back in Ireland, Patrick busied himself with baptizing thousands of people, ordaining priests, and performing conversions. He was a persuasive and evocative speaker—he was famous for using a three-leafed shamrock to demonstrate the idea of the Holy Trinity. Amazingly, he voluntarily returned to the place of his dreaded captivity, based on an inner vision and urging.

Don't discount the power of those voices of instruction that you hear in your head! Sometimes, our minds tell us things that seem startling, out of nowhere, impossible! We owe it to ourselves to listen to our innermost guide, even if what we are hearing surprises or shocks us!

When you hear a calling or come to understand that your help is needed, you may not always enjoy the benefit of St. Patrick's clarity. But emulate his courage and be confident in yourself—the quiet whispers of your spirit can become joyous shouts if the time is right and you feel ready to act!

St. Patrick's memorable sermons were often accompanied by miracles, which only helped his case. According to legend, he rid Ireland of all snakes by chasing them into the sea after they bothered him during a 40-day fast he was doing.

In another episode, St. Patrick rammed his walking stick into the ground while preaching in order to make a point. His crowd proved so skeptical that Patrick kept driving the stick into the ground again and again, until it blossomed into a tree. (No doubt that moment got the crowd's attention!)

St. Patrick is the patron saint of Ireland, Nigeria, Puerto Rico, Boston, and other locations, as well as barbers, blacksmiths, engineers, excluded people, hairdressers, miners, and paralegals.

In art, St. Patrick is usually depicted wearing his bishop's robes, with a harp, shamrock, or cross. He is often portrayed driving snakes before him or trampling upon snakes.

ST. PAUL

What has been the most memorable event in your life? It's probably a moment that is closely tied to your identity. Maybe you remember every detail of the day you met your spouse. Or the day your first child was born. Or the day you got that huge work promotion that meant so much to you!

For many of the saints, the biggest and most powerful moment of their lives could be the occasion of their martyrdom. Other times, it is the moment they perform a huge miracle that drives home their message to a huge crowd. For the 1st-century Roman St. Paul, the defining moment was when he saw the error of his ways—which came with a helpful flesh-and-blood visual!

St. Paul was born in a devout Jewish city, and he was initially named Saul. Saul placed great pride in his Jewish heritage. He boasted, "I am a pure-blooded citizen of Israel and a member of the tribe of Benjamin—a real Hebrew if there ever was one! I was a member of the Pharisees, who demand the strictest obedience to the Jewish law" (Philippians 3:5).

Saul worked as a tent-maker, but his passion was persecution. As a young adult, he would torment and arrest Jesus's early disciples in and around Jerusalem. He also participated in the stoning death of St. Stephen.

One day, while Saul was traveling from Jerusalem to Damascus, he experienced a powerful vision of the resurrected Jesus, bathed in light. Jesus asked Saul why he was persecuting Jesus and his followers.

As Saul and the vision of Jesus conversed on that road, Saul expressed his confusion about Jesus's presence. Jesus explained how damaging Saul's actions were.

After the two parted ways, Saul was struck blind. His loss of sight was immediate—he required a guide in order to walk into Damascus!

For the three days that his blindness lasted, Saul ate and drank nothing. He prayed for hours on end, seeking answers and guidance. Finally, Ananias of Damascus came to Saul and said, "Brother Saul, the Lord Jesus, who appeared to you on the road, has sent me so that you might regain your sight and be filled with the Holy Spirit" (Acts 9:17).

Saul turned on a dime. In fact, Saul became Paul, and as soon as he returned to Jerusalem, began spreading the good news of his vision.

No doubt Paul's three days of blindness and fasting had prepared his mind for a radical new discovery. The only logical thing for him to do then was to act on it!

And that's exactly what he did. Paul underwent a massive conversion and became a new person. People were amazed to see that the man who had spoken out so strongly against Jesus was now calling himself "the servant of Christ"!

Saul was called out! Think of a time you have worked up the nerve to confront someone, or you have been confronted yourself. These are the most uncomfortable kind of conversations!

When we are moved to have this kind of interaction, it is always because the subject is too important to let slide. Jesus must have felt that way about Saul's vehement persecution campaign. At the same time, there's a huge power that comes from admitting our mistakes. How freeing it is to say out loud, or in our hearts, "I was wrong on that one!" and setting out to redeem ourselves.

Just because we have taken the wrong side of the argument at first, it does not invalidate the purity of our intentions or the potency of our thoughts. In fact, being able to understand different, completely opposite points of view is a wonderful quality!

Throughout his adult life, St. Paul traveled far and wide. He is considered to be an extremely influential apostle, and his work was critical in the establishment and spread of Jesus Christ's teachings.

St. Paul drew a lot of attention wherever he went, thanks to the power of his story and the strength of his oratory skills. But with this attention came detractors. Some were upset at his conversion from Judaism. St. Paul was arrested twice—the second time, in Rome in A.D. 67, the insane Emperor Nero ordered his death. Nero may have known him personally.

St. Paul's many miracles are referenced extensively in Scripture. The facts of his three-day blindness and regaining of sight were miraculous. St. Paul brought both old and young people back from the brink of illness and death, as described in the Book of Acts.

Who knows the power of listening better than St. Paul? He is the patron saint of missions, theologians, and Gentile Christians. He is the saint protector of a number of occupations, as well: missionaries and evangelists; writers, journalists, and authors; public workers; and rope, saddle, and tent makers.

We all experience moments of confusion and doubt. And as St. Paul's most memorable moment reminds us, sometimes it's when we feel so sure and secure in our beliefs that we are just about to learn of something that changes everything.

St. Peter

All of us have some "growing pains" on the way to finding the right role for ourselves.

This was a struggle that St. Peter faced. The "Apostle of the Apostles," as he was called, was the first pope, and his influence on the development of the Church and the spread of Christianity was massive.

But even Peter had doubts and failings. A fisherman by trade, St. Peter was named Simon at birth. One day, Simon; his brother Andrew; and Andrew's sons Zebedee, James, and John were standing on the shore of Lake Gennesaret.

On the shore was a huge group of people—Jesus Christ was preaching to an ever-growing crowd, and as the throngs pressed toward him, he was forced to step into a boat, which he used as a makeshift podium to preach from.

Simon and Andrew owned the boat, and they became curious about Jesus. Who was this man, and why was he drawing such large crowds? Meanwhile, the two were having trouble catching any decent number of fish.

Jesus had a suggestion to address this problem. He told Simon and Andrew to dip their nets into the water and reel them back. The brothers were surprised—this was not their usual method of fishing! But they figured there was no harm in humoring this man, so they dropped their nets into the water.

When Simon and Andrew pulled the nets out, they were so full of fish that they had to offload some into a passing boat, and even then both boats were so laden that they could barely float!

Simon started to feel sheepish, frustrated that his previous methods had not been so successful in catching fish. He felt dishonest for taking Jesus's advice and enjoying the fruits of another man's idea.

Jesus put an end to those feelings immediately. He showed Simon the bigger picture by telling him that now Simon would trade in his fisherman occupation in order to be a "fisher of men."

Jesus gave Simon more guidance when he renamed him Peter. As they discussed Jesus's vision for his apostle's ministry, Jesus praised his faith, telling him that he would be the rock on which his entire church was built. And Jesus called him "Peter," from the Greek word for rock.

Despite their rich history as mutual supporters and collaborators, St. Peter famously denied Jesus three times—even after he witnessed Jesus walking on water and stayed by Jesus's side for the travels and teachings of his miraculous life. During the Last Supper, Jesus predicted this—he told Peter that he would deny him three times before the rooster crowed twice.

Sure enough, St. Peter did as Jesus predicted, denying he had been with Jesus when a servant asked him, again when the same servant told passersby that Peter was a disciple of Jesus, and once more when someone heard Peter's accent and asked him if he was a follower of Jesus.

What can account for these moments of weakness? It wasn't as if St. Peter slipped once—he denied Jesus three times, on separate occasions, and even after he had been explicitly told that it would happen!

We are only human, and emotions like fear, confusion, and self-preservation are natural. St. Peter felt another very human emotion after his denials and after Jesus's crucifixion—guilt.

Unverified legend says that when St. Peter was sentenced to death in A.D. 64 by Emperor Nero, he was so guilt-ridden about his denial of Jesus that he refused to be executed in the same way. The legend says that St. Peter was crucified upside down—an enduring image of art and metaphor.

Hold your relationships dear, and appreciate your mentors and friends. But when human doubts muddy things, do not fear! There is no need to beat yourself up.

This is a very relatable feeling. Have you ever struggled to do something your way, only to receive seemingly counterintuitive guidance from someone else? You may have resisted taking the advice, but then you may have finally tried it. Did it work? How did that make you feel—like you had banged your head against the wall for ages trying to find a solution, only for someone to walk by casually and get it right!

Simon felt the same way, but Jesus gave him a pep talk! Doesn't it feel wonderful to receive a "vote of confidence" from those who know us best? When you do hear such kind words, don't sell yourself short! Take a moment to appreciate the love that others are showing you through their faith in you. You are a vital figure in someone's plans! Our relationships are the sum of our greatest moments, not of our temporary lows.

St. Peter is the patron saint of popes, roosters, bakers, butchers, bridge builders, fishermen, harvesters, watchmakers, locksmiths, cobblers, shipwrights, and stationers.

St. Philomena

Who is your cheerleader?

Celebrities have publicists, who make a life of sharing their clients' good work. Politicians have a press secretary, who carefully manages news stories. It's so important to have an advocate who can speak up about your good works and set the record straight!

Saints need cheerleaders, too. The process of nomination, beatification, and canonization is long and complicated. And most saints are alike in life in that they have been humble, hardworking, and reluctant to draw attention to themselves!

St. Philomena was a young consecrated virgin whose biography is uncertain. Though she was born around the 3rd century in Corfu, Greece, her remains were accidentally discovered centuries later, in 1802. The excavation of her grave site spurred a reexamination of St. Philomena's life.

How great it is when we have the opportunity to take a "second look" at something that deserves our attention. This blessing of rediscovery coincided with the life of a 19th-century Italian nun who took up Philomena's banner.

The story of St. Philomena cannot be unbound from that of Sister Maria Luisa di Gesù. Sister Maria Luisa was a Dominican tertiary from Naples who said she was visited by the spirit of St. Philomena. Her inspiration to tell the world Philomena's story led to the recognition of this virgin martyr as a saint.

According to Sister Maria Luisa's account, St. Philomena was a Greek princess born into a pagan family, but who converted to Christianity along with her mother. At 13, Philomena took a vow of consecrated virginity. This did not go over well at all—the Emperor Diocletian, who was firmly anti-Christian, threatened to declare war if Philomena and her mother did not abandon their Christian beliefs.

Philomena and her parents traveled to visit Emperor Diocletian to see if they could spread the love of God to him in person. But Diocletian fell in love with St. Philomena at first sight and demanded that she marry him. She refused, of course, and the cruel emperor subjected her to a series of increasingly horrific tortures, including scourging, tying her to an anchor and throwing her into the river, shooting her with arrows, and finally decapitation.

For all but the final torture, angels intervened in order to spare St. Philomena the pain and trauma of her treatment. When Philomena was decapitated, it was at 3 P.M. on a Friday—the same day and time as Jesus's death.

The story outlined for St. Philomena's life is similar to that of many other virgin martyrs. Philomena was certain of her devotion to God, but she lived in a time in which she was supposed to renounce that faith or conceal it from the public. She did neither, and she faced further challenges in preserving her vow of virginity.

Centuries after both St. Philomena's death and the time of Sister Maria Luisa—the woman who shared her story with the world—Philomena's canonization was called into question. While the lack of hard evidence led the Holy See to remove her name from official local calendars, it does not diminish the power of her story or even her standing as a saint.

Beautiful, young, and pure St. Philomena is often depicted carrying her palm of martyrdom or wearing a flower crown. She is shown in orange or white robes frequently, sometimes pierced with arrows, tied to an anchor, or with a partially slit throat.

St. Philomena suffered silently in life, and she almost remained silent after her death, too. She is the patron saint of infants, children, and youth; priests; lost causes; virgins; and the sterile.

Do you have a problem that you feel nobody can help with or even properly hear you on, like the devout Philomena appealing to the pagan emperor? Have you ever fought an uphill battle to convince people of something, with little evidence available to help in your quest, like Sister Maria Luisa? Sometimes it can feel like you're going crazy as you insist on some fact—and all the while people stare at you like you have two heads!

Life—and not only spiritual life—is filled with moments where we have to "refill" our faith all by ourselves. You may face doubts and criticisms, but do not let those negative words stop you from accomplishing the work that you know in your heart you are meant to do!

ST. RITA OF CASCIA

Have you ever had the kind of day where everything goes wrong? The kind that is just so bad that you laugh and wonder, *Why can't I catch a break?!*

Highs and lows in life help remind us how blessed we are. Ups and downs give us perspective.

However bad your worst day was, hopefully it wasn't anything like the series of misfortunes that St. Rita of Cascia suffered during a life filled with hardship, uncertainty, and abuse. But each trial she endured only made her more sure in her faith, and more devoted in her worship.

St. Rita of Cascia was born Margherita Lotti in late 14th-century Italy. Her mother and father, Antonio and Amata Ferri Lotti, were well-born and charitable. While the family was not overtly religious, her parents' passion for service and volunteering had a strong impact on Rita.

Rita became interested in pursuing a spiritual life early on, but her parents objected to the practical realities of such a plan. Marriage was "the thing to do" in her time and society; less traditional options like joining a nunnery did not sit well with Antonia and Amata.

Rita's parents married her off to a nobleman named Paolo Mancini, who was a good match on paper. But Paolo's temper, combined with Rita's complete lack of interest in even being married, made for a tumultuous union. (Not to mention the fact that she was only 12 at the time of her wedding!)

Throughout an 18-year marriage, Paolo cheated on Rita, and he verbally and physically abused her. But she treated her husband with kindness, patience, and understanding, and through her example, she changed him into a nicer, gentler man. They had two children, Giangiacomo Antonio and Paulo Maria, who were raised Christian.

Rita's husband softened greatly over time, as a direct result of Rita's vast influence. But unfortunately, Paolo's "softness" indirectly led to his being killed! When Paolo and Rita first got married, his family was involved in a bitter family feud called *la Vendetta*.

Over nearly two decades, Rita had taught Paolo how to get past the feud and move toward love and acceptance. Paolo did just that, but nobody else involved in the feud shared this view. As a result, Paolo was double-crossed by those whom he naively trusted, and he was stabbed to death.

Tragedy continued to follow Rita years later, when both her sons died of dysentery. The grieving mother sought to enter the monastery of St. Mary Magdalene in Cascia—she had always desired a religious life, and this tragic moment offered a unique opportunity to fulfill her calling.

Unfortunately, the monastery refused to accept Rita due to her not being a virgin! The nuns also cited the scandal of her husband's violent death, which they believed would cause the wrong kind of attention for their quiet religious order.

Rita would not give up her dream so easily. She continued to campaign the monastery until they relented, on one condition. Rita would have to achieve the seemingly impossible task of securing peace between the feuding families.

Just as in all times of torment or trouble, Rita prayed for help, and a truce was reached. The monastery relented, and at long last, she became a nun as a 36-year-old widow.

Though she had loved and lost, and endured great trials and sadness at this relatively young age, St. Rita was never more content than when she finally entered a life devoted to religious practice. Several miracles occurred while she was in the monastery.

When she was about 60 years old, Rita noticed a small knot on her forehead, which seemed to poke through her flesh as a "thorn" from Christ's crown. This mark remained for the next 15 years of her life, a sign of her deep connection and devotion to Christ.

At the end of her life, Rita was bedridden at the convent when another miracle occurred. A visiting cousin asked if she could bring the elderly nun anything. Rita said she wanted a rose from the garden. It was January and the ground was frozen solid, yet when the cousin went home, she found a single blooming rose, which she brought back. This is why Rita is often depicted holding roses or standing among blooms.

St. Rita of Cascia is the patron saint of family honor and difficult marriages. It seems St. Rita is the embodiment of the old saying, "turn lemons into lemonade"! There seems to be no situation in her life that turned out how she initially desired. And there also seems to be no situation that she didn't improve with her gentle faith and patient charity.

When you envision your life, you surely don't ask for hardship. But as you look at the courageous example of St. Rita of Cascia, take heart—though suffering is not pleasant, it is the surest way to grow our faith and improve ourselves.

St. Sebastian

We all endure emotional challenges every day. Perhaps we feel "picked on"—like nobody understands where we're coming from or what we have to offer. Maybe we feel that our blessings and our passions can't truly be appreciated in the environment we find ourselves in.

Think of a time when you have pushed yourself to the limit to fulfill your obligations, but you were "punished" for your good deeds. However you felt in this situation, do not internalize it! Your worth and your power extend so far beyond the "slings and arrows" that may be directed at you.

Nothing demonstrates this idea of a piercing assault more clearly than the story of St. Sebastian. Even if his name doesn't ring a bell, you may have encountered his very memorable likeness in art: He is the saint often shown stuck through with arrows, like a pincushion!

And the amazing thing is that he survived that episode in his life! If you are feeling discouraged, then think about that improbable fact.

Sebastian was born in mid-3rd-century Rome. An able-bodied and well-educated man, he joined the Roman army. He was a natural fit, with his peak athletic condition and measured personality. He rose quickly to the rank of captain of the Praetorian Guard.

But St. Sebastian had a secret: He served at the pleasure of Emperor Diocletian, a leader who was famous for his persecution of Christians, yet he himself was extremely devout.

St. Sebastian did his best to continue doing his job while staying true to his spiritual beliefs. One of his major tasks for the emperor was rounding up Christians and sending them to prison. Instead of focusing on finding Christians, Sebastian used his patrols to find nonbelievers, and then he showed them the love of God. Many converted on the spot.

By 286, Sebastian's good works caught up with him—Emperor Diocletian summoned him to his court, and told him he felt "betrayed" by his captain's covert conversion missions. As punishment, Sebastian was taken out to an open field and tied to a post, where archers were invited to use him for target practice.

After the cruel archers departed the field that night and left the terribly wounded St. Sebastian for dead, they were in for quite a surprise! A woman, Irene of Rome, was sent to retrieve St. Sebastian's corpse the next day and prepare it for burial, but she found, to her shock and amazement, that Sebastian was still alive.

And it wasn't just his body. Amazingly, after that terrible ordeal, Sebastian's belief in fighting for goodness was intact, too! After being untied, he wasted no time in seeking out Emperor Diocletian. He wanted to confront his tormentor—even though his tormentor was the most powerful man in the Roman Empire!

Sebastian gained an audience with Diocletian, probably more to satisfy the emperor's morbid curiosity than anything else. Sebastian didn't mince words—he told Diocletian how wrong he was for persecuting Christians.

In addition to his astonishment that Sebastian hadn't died, Diocletian was surprised, to say the least, by Sebastian's enduring faith. But once he recovered from this, he ordered his henchmen to finish the job—Sebastian was beaten to death with cudgels and thrown into a sewer.

St. Sebastian's bodily strength and endurance are rivaled only by his mental courage and moral purity.

Do you need assistance in a situation where you feel powerful opposition? His remarkable story is a great inspiration for all those who must go up against great odds. He is the patron saint of soldiers, archers, holy Christian death, athletes, and the plague stricken.

Can you think of a time when, like St. Sebastian, you were called to do important work, but the demands of your task required you to cooperate with people you felt at odds with? It's very common—whether in social groups, families, or occupations. Your passion and the strength of your convictions will carry the day.

While it's fair to say that most of us have not been used as archery targets before (thank goodness!), we can all relate to the feeling of being under suspicion and attack. Think of a time when you did everything you could to be a force for good but seemed to get nothing but pushback in response! Let go of any negative feelings about that difficult moment. And think of the power of St. Sebastian's example. He reminds us that we may encounter the harshest of obstacles when we try to be a force for good. Do not let those arrows stop you!

Because when you are truly on right path, and secure in the worthiness of your mission, the arrows that the world seems to be shooting at you are really just directional pointers. The weapons of attack that your detractors let loose on you are in fact pointing toward the great light and power that is coming from inside you, impervious to outside assaults.

ST. TERESA OF ÁVILA

How can you hope to get anything done when worldly distractions are pulling at you? Even a person of great spiritual discipline and superhuman concentration couldn't help but be distracted by the extra "noise" of the outside world!

But as you will see from the story of St. Teresa of Ávila—Spanish mystic, Carmelite nun, and scholarly author for the Counter-Reformation—it is possible to amass great accomplishments and do great and powerful work to protect the sanctity of your spiritual practice.

Born 1515 in Ávila, Spain, Teresa came from a family that had already suffered religious persecution. Her grandparents were Jewish converts to Christianity who had been questioned and condemned during the Spanish Inquisition. Because of this background, her parents were very aware of the need to assimilate during tumultuous political times, while also spreading the love and light of their deeply held religious beliefs.

Teresa developed an early fascination with saints and martyrdom. All around her, she heard stories of the difficulties that religious visionaries had suffered, just for standing up for their beliefs. She began to feel a responsibility to speak out in her own time.

When Teresa was 14, her mother passed away suddenly. Grief caused her to seek deeper meaning, and take comfort, in her spirituality. She adopted the Virgin Mary as a kind of surrogate mother figure, and she was sent away to be educated by Augustinian nuns in Ávila.

Her time in the monastery led to even greater reflection and spiritual awakening. While reading a devotional work called the *Third Spiritual Alphabet*, Teresa kept experiencing bouts of extreme religious ecstasy. These episodes grew from her love of meditation and contemplation, and according to Teresa's account, they culminated in a perfect union with God, during which she received a "blessing of tears."

Teresa reported a vision of Jesus Christ himself in 1559, and she said these spiritual visitations continued daily for two years. On another occasion, an angel came down to her and pierced her heart with a golden arrow! This inspired her to keep pursuing mortification and suffering, in the hopes of drawing closer to the divine.

Upon entering a Carmelite monastery in 1535, Teresa looked around and found herself dismayed. With her history of divine visions, and with all the time she had spent in conversation with and reflection upon God, she felt quite disappointed by how that compared with the worldliness of monastic life.

For example, the practice of *cloistering*—meaning nuns would be kept separate from the outside world—was enforced in an erratic and haphazard way at her monastery. Political bigwigs and other secular characters would stream into the monastery constantly, motivated by a desire to socialize and dabble rather than to understand the divine.

And so Teresa began a reform campaign that ended up revolutionizing her entire orbit. With the backing of a wealthy friend, she created a new Carmelite convent. This new convent would be a refuge of sorts, where the laxness of her former monastery would be addressed and corrected. Teresa tightened up the exercise of cloistering, and she announced a rule of absolute poverty in the convent.

St. Teresa was a thinker and a feeler. She is the patron saint of lace makers, chess, people in need of grace, the sick, and those ridiculed for their piety.

If you have ever felt that you've had valuable contributions to make in a flawed system, then Teresa of Ávila is the saint for you to look to. As a visionary and mystic, she was skilled at seeing the potential in the future, not the limitations of the present.

If your goals are creative and innovative, then you may encounter an amazing amount of resistance and naysaying, just as Teresa had to contend with. The greatest and most revolutionary ideas can seem crazy up until the moment they are put in place—and then they seem like the most logical and natural thing in the world.

St. Thérèse of Lisieux

Quality over quantity.

That's a major theme in the life and philosophy of St. Thérèse of Lisieux, also known as the Little Flower, one of the most well-known and popular saints in the canon.

What was so inspiring about this young girl, who spent less than a decade involved in formal religious work? Her spirit and deeds—as captured vividly in her posthumously published autobiography *The Story of a Soul*—offer a message that's completely universal.

"My way is all confidence and love." That's Thérèse's spirit in one sentence. The line comes from *The Story of a Soul*, which was pieced together from journal entries, letters, and notes. The autobiography was published with little fanfare in 1898, one year after Thérèse's death at age 24.

Thérèse was born in 1873 to a watchmaker father and a lace-maker mother in Lisieux, France. The couple had nine children, though only five lived to become adults. Thérèse was the youngest of the big brood, and in her early years, she was pampered and indulged.

When her mother died suddenly when Thérèse was only four years old, the family grew closer as all the siblings and their father banded together to make ends meet. Thérèse's older sister Pauline became something of a surrogate mother figure, instilling a deep love for religion in Thérèse. Pauline read religious stories to her siblings and made sure that they were educated about spiritual matters. When Pauline left to join a Carmelite convent several years later, the nine-year-old Thérèse openly admired her sister and declared her own plans to follow Pauline's path.

There was one small problem: Thérèse was quick-tempered and sensitive to perceived slights. Due to a lifetime of being treated as the "baby," Thérèse had trouble feeling empathy for others.

This manifested in tantrums, screaming outbursts, and crying fits when she felt she was being criticized.

Thérèse turned to Jesus for help with the outbursts. She knew her goal, and she knew why she wasn't fit to reach it yet—but she was unable to take that last step and improve her own behaviors. She grew even more frustrated as she realized that she was being her own worst enemy!

Thérèse's prayers were answered when she was 14 years old. According to a longstanding family tradition, Thérèse's sisters would leave gifts in her shoes each Christmas morning. It was a ritual that had started when Thérèse was a baby, but Thérèse's father felt that at 14, she was too old for this treatment. More importantly, he suspected—correctly so—that all the attention was making Thérèse a bit spoiled and self-centered.

On Christmas Day in 1886, Thérèse's father noticed the gifts in shoes for Thérèse and yelled out in frustration. Everyone expected Thérèse to scream back in retaliation or burst into tears. But she didn't. Just like that, the "change" that Thérèse had prayed for came into her heart. It was like a bolt of lightning, and she instantly understood why her father was frustrated. While she felt excitement and anticipation about the presents, she suddenly realized that her own feelings were not necessarily universal—and that she had a duty to consider the comfort of others.

For the first time in her young life, she remained calm and mature during the outburst. Describing the incident in her journal (and, later, her autobiography), Thérèse called this moment "The Complete Conversion," after which her divine path was firmly fixed. When Christmas Day came around the next year, the gifts-in-shoes debate was irrelevant—Thérèse had moved out of the house and joined a Carmelite convent.

Six years into her career at the Carmel of Lisieux, Thérèse felt as though she had hit a wall. She entered with huge ambitions: She wanted to be a saint. But as she evaluated her own heart day after day, she felt small and insignificant. She wasn't the type to put on flashy displays or perform impressively miraculous feats.

Further, she struggled to consistently fulfill even the mental components of her quest. Since the Complete Conversion, her outbursts had been drastically reduced. But they hadn't been eliminated. Thérèse recognized that she wasn't perfect. She was very much human. And she was starting to feel deeply discouraged.

That's when she discovered two passages from the Bible that inspired her. The first was Proverbs 9:4 (ESV), which says: "Whoever is simple, let him turn in here." The second was Isaiah 66:12–13 (ESV), which says: "you shall be carried upon her hip, and bounced upon her knees. As one whom his mother comforts, so I will comfort you."

She had her answer! Thérèse interpreted these excerpts as confirmation that small works can add up to something huge. Writing about her newly formed philosophy in her journal, Thérèse noted that anyone can perform such little deeds. Greatness comes from the heart.

St. Thérèse is credited with at least two miraculous cures—to help rid a St. Germain woman of deadly stomach ulcers in 1913 and clear a young seminarian of his advanced pulmonary tuberculosis.

St. Thérèse is the patron saint of the gardens at the Vatican, sufferers of HIV/AIDS and tuberculosis, missionaries, Alaska, France, florists, and orphans. Her attributes include roses, the crucifix, and her traditional Carmelite habit.

Have you ever doubted your ability to make an impact? Have you felt insignificant and small? Take heart! St. Thérèse is a wonderful role model when you feel your faith is wavering or you fear that your best efforts will not be good enough. She offers a reminder that when your heart belongs to Jesus, you are much more powerful than you realize. She compared tiny acts of love and devotion to "little flowers." The smallest blooms can brighten up even a massive field.

St. Thomas Aquinas

"Be reasonable!"

Are you a thinker? Do you have an analytical mind? If you have ever told someone to "be reasonable," then you are capturing the heart of St. Thomas Aquinas's quest. He was a hugely influential 13th-century saint who loved to both learn and teach. Through his passion for philosophy, theology, and academics, he embraced the power of logic. He was famous for saying that reason is found in God.

From an early age, Thomas Aquinas demonstrated his love for giving things due consideration. Born into a wealthy family in medieval Sicily, Thomas Aquinas was expected to follow his uncle's career path of abbot. Beginning when he was five years old, Thomas studied at the abbey at Monte Cassino.

But his education was disrupted when a military conflict between Emperor Frederick II and Pope Gregory IX shattered the peace of the abbey, forcing Thomas's parents to move him to another school.

At Thomas's new school, he studied the great philosophers Aristotle, Averroes, and Maimonides. And in this new environment, he realized he wanted to pursue philosophical thought himself.

There was another key event that happened at Thomas's new school—the young student met a preacher named John of St. Julian, an active recruiter for a new Dominican order. Thomas was intrigued by what John of St. Julian told him about the Dominicans, but he knew that his parents had very specific plans for him that were not compatible with the wonderful things he was hearing about from the preacher.

At 19, Thomas ripped the bandage off, so to speak. He revealed to his parents his new plan: He didn't want to follow his uncle's path to become an abbot. Instead, he hoped to join the new Dominican order.

This news didn't sit well with Thomas's family at all. Who could blame them? They had pinned so many hopes on Thomas and their plans for his entire life. They, like any parents, only wanted what was best for him. But despite his respect for their desires, Thomas heard a loud call, and he could not ignore it.

When Thomas set out for Paris to join the Dominicans, his parents intercepted him and brought him back home by force. They kept him against his will at the family castle, hoping that time and captivity would change his mind about his plan to join the Dominicans.

Over two years of captivity, Thomas's family grew increasingly desperate when they saw that his will could not be bent. His brothers even hired a prostitute to try to seduce him and turn him from his celibate path, but Thomas chased the woman away with an iron from the fire.

When it became clear that Thomas's plans could not be changed, his parents decided to let him leave the castle to join the Dominicans. However, his mother did not want the embarrassment of having to explain that she had locked her son up for years, only to relent and send him off to the Dominican order against the family's wishes. So she arranged for Thomas to flee the castle (with her assistance) under cover of night so that everyone could save face.

After he finally joined the Dominican order, St. Thomas began a highly productive career as a teacher, philosopher, and writer of religious works. He was a man of few words. In fact, he spoke so little that others at the monastery thought he might be mentally delayed. But the Dominican scholar Albertus Magnus said of him: "You call him the dumb ox, but in his teaching he will one day produce such a bellowing that it will be heard throughout the world."

How true this statement was! Even if you are not a follower or a fan of St. Thomas Aquinas and his writings, we have all benefited from the love of inquiry and debate that he promoted through his works. He is the patron saint of students, apologists, book sellers, schools, chastity, learning, pencil makers, philosophers, and publishers.

Even if you are not a student, there is always so much to learn in life. Never stop pursuing new information and new discoveries. And do not hesitate to fight for your future. Even though your loved ones may not agree with your vision at first, the light in you is great. The strength of your passion will see you to your goal!

ST. THOMAS MORE

Have you ever had an experience where you idolized someone or something until you got a closer look?

This is a common danger for analytical people, or "overthinkers"! Sometimes our illusions are shattered as we grow older and take our "blinders" off, suddenly seeing the failings of our heroes—or our monarchs.

This theme fits in well with the life of St. Thomas More. Highly educated, he was a great example of a "Renaissance man." Thomas More was a trained lawyer, philosopher, writer, statesman, and scholar in 15th- and 16th-century England. He had elite political connections stemming from his education, nobility, and occupation. King Henry VIII held St. Thomas More as a close confidant, valuing his levelheaded analysis. Unfortunately, it was St. Thomas More's intellect and his logic that caused the vengeful king to eventually sentence him to death.

Thomas More was born to a high-ranking judge, Sir John More, and his wife, Agnes. He attended all the top schools, and after his education, he entered the fast track to a great career serving high-ranking officials. After a stint working for the Archbishop of Canterbury, Thomas went to study at Oxford. His Oxford tenure only lasted a couple of years. At his father's urging, Thomas pursued a career as a lawyer, moving to London for law school.

London was a very secular place then, as it is now. Nevertheless, the young Thomas found himself exploring religion more and more. While at law school, Thomas heavily considered dropping out and becoming a monk. His school dormitory was near a Carthusian monastery, and Thomas loved nothing better than to join the monks during their spiritual exercises. He had a rather intellectual appreciation for the discipline and stoicism of the monks.

In his early adulthood, Thomas became a lawyer, an elected Parliament representative, and secretary and personal advisor to

King Henry VIII. It was in this last role that he saw an opportunity for great influence.

For Thomas, the most important cause while he served on the king's court was religion. The Protestant Reformation was gaining traction, and Thomas was a purist who viewed the movement as threatening to the very fabric of society.

Times were hard in Thomas's England. Religious strife was tearing across the country, and as an official employee of the king, Thomas found himself in a difficult position. He was called to walk a delicate diplomatic line—which is why he is considered the patron saint of politicians and statesman!

His formerly close relationship with King Henry VIII started to crumble when the king decided to divorce his wife, Catherine of Aragon. The king faced a bit of a PR nightmare with his plans to remarry. Disillusioned with Henry, Thomas refused to be a yes-man—he found the remarriage idea to be quite distasteful and hypocritical.

But like anyone in this era, Thomas understood what it meant to speak out against the king. You couldn't really defy the most powerful man in England and live to tell about it.

Indeed, St. Thomas More was arrested for treason and held in the Tower of London. While there, he wrote his devotional *Dialogue of Comfort Against Tribulation*. Following a short trial and an even shorter jury deliberation—only 15 minutes—St. Thomas More was found guilty and sentenced to death.

As Thomas More's inspiring life shows us, we owe it to ourselves to think hard about our path and our choices. Think of a time when you felt caught in the middle. The middle is the least comfortable place to be. You can sometimes feel like two sides are playing tug-of-war and you are the rope! It's even worse when one of the sides pulling at you is your boss and sovereign, as was the case with St. Thomas More. Yet he did not take the path of least resistance, and neither should you.

The next time you are struggling to make a point, do not be discouraged. Think of St. Thomas More—the patron saint of adopted children, civil servants, court clerks, difficult marriages, large families, lawyers, widowers, and stepparents—and you will remember that though the stakes may be high and the task may be difficult, it is always important to speak up!

ST. VALENTINE

Do you have people in your life you never expected to be friends with? When you diversify your close circle, it helps you gain much-needed perspective. And your friends are gaining valuable perspective from you, too! Our lives are enriched by our relationships with people we may never have been drawn to otherwise or who hold divergent beliefs.

This was the case with St. Valentine, one of the most widely known Roman martyrs, born and executed in the 3rd century. While the details of his life are uncertain, he has been depicted quite frequently in legends and artwork, and is closely associated with romantic love—and with a holiday that many people celebrate. If you have ever exchanged candy or flowers on February 14, perhaps you gave a passing thought to St. Valentine. But how does his life tie into our beliefs about love?

According to the most popular story, St. Valentine was a Roman priest. He lived in a society that was considered highly modern—but it was also largely pagan. In his work and through his social status, St. Valentine encountered many high-ranking officials, and he always used these opportunities to share his beliefs on Christianity and try to spread the light of spirituality to the pagan Romans.

Eventually, Valentine was placed under arrest by Judge Asterius for his preaching. The two began discussing Christianity, and the judge was intrigued. But he wanted proof of all the great things St. Valentine was talking about.

The judge brought his blind daughter, Julia, to St. Valentine. St. Valentine—a kindhearted and empathetic man—formed a tender friendship with Julia. He spoke with her and listened to her stories. One day, when St. Valentine wished to leave a kind note, or "valentine," to Julia, he wrote on a scrap of paper, handed it to her, and touched her eyes. Thanks to the power of his kindness, and due to Julia's desire to see her friend's note, she regained her vision—permanently!

For St. Valentine, this was a big moment. Because of this incident, the judge was eager to listen to St. Valentine's teachings. He was quite ready to learn!

So St. Valentine told the judge that he should destroy all the pagan idols around his house, fast for three days, and then undergo a baptism. When the judge fulfilled this request, there was a further positive impact—now that he was converted, he felt sympathy for all the Christians he had persecuted, and he freed the religious prisoners under his authority.

Talk about using momentum to your advantage! This was one of the many heroic acts that St. Valentine accomplished during his short but eventful life.

But because St. Valentine lived in a time of high hostility toward Christians, he wasn't home free just because he had converted the judge. He continuing spreading his love for Christ through Rome, and he was arrested once more for this crime.

This time, St. Valentine's luck wouldn't hold—he was arrested by the emperor himself, Claudius Gothicus, and the emperor was not so open to conversion. He told St. Valentine that he had two choices: (1) renounce his Christianity, or (2) be beaten and killed.

Since St. Valentine refused to take the first option, he was executed on the emperor's command.

If you are wondering how a martyred saint became connected with the most romantic holiday—legend says that St. Valentine loved nothing better than to marry young couples. Marriage was one of the sacred institutions in Christianity, but pagans didn't share this priority. By promoting wedded unions, St. Valentine gently spread his message of Christianity and sacred love.

Think of a time when, like St. Valentine, you have proved your doubters wrong. Oh, it is so human to think *I told you so!* or feel pride at these moments. But beyond that natural impulse, how did you use this moment to push forward with your work?

Aside from his spectacular and well-known miracle of helping a blind woman to see, Valentine has been credited with helping many others. He is the patron saint of engaged couples, beekeepers, happy marriages, love, the plague stricken, and epileptics.

St. Valentine is often depicted with birds and roses, or in the presence of crippled or epileptic children. Sometimes he is shown at the most famous moments of his life—teaching his countrymen that they should not worship idols, or restoring a young girl's vision. Other times, he is shown marrying young couples. Weddings were a key part of St. Valentine's conversion strategy—it was a "soft sell" through which he could expose people to the awesome power of love.

St. Valentine showed the Romans how love for your fellow man flows out of the same fountain that our love for God does. Think of him next time you enjoy a heart-shaped piece of chocolate on Valentine's Day!

AFTERWORD

HONORING SAINTS AND ANGELS AND PRAYING TO GOD

Regarding saints, as you know, we don't pray to them—yet for me, saints are inspiring for their earthly stories. Who isn't inspired by the beloved and heroic story of St. Francis, Joan of Arc, or St. Bernadette?

Similarly, we're told not to pray to angels, although we can certainly venerate and appreciate God's holy angels. Just as it is important to understand *how* God wants us to pray, it's also important to know to whom we're *not* supposed to pray. There are various religions and paths that promote praying to saints, angels, dead relatives, and other deities, but the Word of God does not support this.

This passage from John the Beloved, mentioned in Part II, says it best:

> I, John, am the one who heard and saw all these things. And when I heard and saw them, I fell down to worship at the feet of the angel who showed them to me. But he said, "No, don't worship me. I am a servant of God, just like you and your brothers the prophets, as well as all who obey what is written in this book. Worship only God!" (Revelation 22:8–9)

That's my experience, too, with angels. They don't want to be worshipped! They give all glory to God, for whom they tirelessly work. You can definitely ask God to send you angels, and you can talk with angels. But please don't worship them.

God desires to be glorified by his children, and praying to angels, deities, and saints would ultimately give them glory over God. Therefore, he desires to be the object of your prayer time. To that end, in the Appendix, I've included example prayers you can direct to God, organized by topic for ease of reference.

As you learned in Part I, there are various Scripture passages that teach that God is three Persons and each holds different attributes of God. It is my prayer that you've been able to learn more about the Holy Trinity—as well as the angels of heaven and the saints who led godly lives on Earth—and that you have grown closer to God as Father, Jesus, and Spirit.

There is only one God, but God is three Persons. Dear one, we have the privilege of getting to know each Person of the Trinity on an individual and intimate level. Maybe you've been outside the Christian faith for a while, or perhaps you've never walked the Christian path. I support you as you earnestly seek the Lord, for he is a loving Father who desires to guide, care for, protect, and love you with the kind of love that your soul has been longing for.

Take time to cultivate a personal relationship with God, Jesus, and Spirit just as you would take time to do so with a new friend. Test it out, as I'm confident that as you seek a greater intimacy with the Holy Trinity, along with the angels and the saints who serve God, you will certainly find it!

BLESSINGS,

Doreen

APPENDIX

PRAYERS FOR PARTICULAR TOPICS

The following are some examples of prayers to start your conversation with God about your situation, alphabetized by topic, with accompanying scriptural verses. Pour your heart out and tell God about everything you're experiencing—your hopes, fears, doubts, and desires.

God already knows what's in your heart, and delights when you bring it to him with the full faith that he will help you. Use your own words for your prayers, expanding these example prayers to fit your particular circumstances.

If you're ever unsure of how to pray, remember to talk with God as you would speak to a beloved parent whom you highly respect—with truth, reverence, and love. These prayers are based upon trusting God's will, and aligning your own will with his.

Career

Dear God,
I know you are my real boss and employer,
and I turn to you for guidance about my career,
so that I can be the most helpful in a meaningful way.
I trust that you supply my earthly needs while I focus upon
listening to and following your guidance.

And may the Lord our God show his approval
and make our efforts successful.
Yes, make our efforts successful!

PSALM 90:17

Children

Dear God,
Thank you for the children of the world,
and for the children you have entrusted to my care.
You are the greatest parent of them all, and I ask that you
inspire my parenting abilities as well. Thank you for helping me
to be a loving, caring, and wise caretaker of children.

Children are a gift from the Lord.

PSALM 127:3

Dating

Dear God,
You who are love and who know all hearts:
Please help me to be in a healthy and equally yoked
romantic relationship, with a partner who is supportive,
trustworthy, and godly. You know who is best for me,
and I need your help, Lord, to hear and follow your guidance.
Please help me to trust and to fully love,
instead of fall prey to my fears and worries.

Don't team up with those who are unbelievers.
How can righteousness be a partner with wickedness?
How can light live with darkness?
. . . How can a believer be a partner with an unbeliever?

2 CORINTHIANS 6:14–15

Family Concerns

Dear God,
You know how much I love my family,
and I'm upset about [describe situation].
Please, Lord, can you intervene to bring about solutions
and peace to our family? I pray that your love will help us
resolve this situation, and bring us closer.

As for me and my family, we will serve the Lord.

JOSHUA 24:15

Financial Needs

Dear God,
You know my needs, and I trust in you providing for me.
Here is the situation that's heavy on my heart: [describe].
Please, Lord, I need your help! Please clearly guide me
so that I can do my part in resolving this.

*Seek the Kingdom of God above all else, and live righteously,
and he will give you everything you need.*

M ATTHEW 6:33

Friendship

Dear God,
I am evolving and changing as I grow closer
to you, and I pray to have friends who also love you.
I pray to foster healthy friendships that are based upon
love and mutual respect. Please, Lord, guide me
to find good friends, and help me to be
a good friend to them, too.

*The godly give good advice to their friends;
the wicked lead them astray.*

P ROVERBS 12:26

Healing, Emotional

Dear God,
My heart hurts from [describe situation],
and I am coming to you for solace, healing, and comfort.
Must I hurt this way, Lord? Could you please help me find relief
from this suffering? I trust that whatever you lead me to
is the way that I am supposed to follow.

The Lord is close to the brokenhearted;
he rescues those whose spirits are crushed.

PSALM 34:18

Healing, Physical

Dear God,
You who made me, you who are the great physician,
please come to my aid with [describe your health situation].
I am clinging to you, in need of your help, Lord.
What should I do to recover my health?
- Please clearly guide me, God.

Dear friend, I hope all is well with you and that
you are as healthy in body as you are strong in spirit.

3 JOHN 1:2

Healing, Relationships

Dear God,
What I am to do about this relationship?
How am I to proceed? Please, Lord, I need your help
and guidance about what to do. I ask that you soften my heart
and the heart of my partner, and guide our conversations
and actions to align with one another.

Love is patient and kind.
Love is not jealous or boastful or proud or rude.
It does not demand its own way. It is not irritable,
and it keeps no record of being wronged.

1 CORINTHIANS 13:4–5

Healthful Eating

Dear God,
I know that you made my body for health and vitality.
Please, Lord, help me with the self-control fruit of your Spirit.
Please guide my appetite and my eating, so that I am taking care
of my body as a temple where your Spirit dwells.

So whether you eat or drink, or whatever
you do, do it all for the glory of God.

1 CORINTHIANS 10:31

Increasing Your Faith

Dear God,
I know that trusting you and having faith are keys
to everything that is good. And yet I admit that at times,
my faith wavers and doubt enters into my mind and heart.
I need your help, Lord, and I know that you can work wonders
in helping me to increase my faith. Please shift me from
doubt to knowingness, and from worry to faith.

*"Dear woman," Jesus said to her,
"your faith is great. Your request is granted."*

MATTHEW 15:28

Job Interview

Dear God,
If this is the right job for me,
please guide my words and actions
with your confidence, grace, and poise.
If this is not the right job for me, please guide me
to the best place for me to work.

*Blessed are those who trust in the Lord
and have made the Lord their hope and confidence.*

JEREMIAH 17:7

Legal Issues

Dear God,
Please shield, defend, and protect me
during [describe the situation]. Please, Lord,
I need your help, and I appeal to you to bolster my strength
and courage. Please show me the best way to proceed.

*But in that coming day no weapon turned against you will
succeed. You will silence every voice raised up to accuse you.*

ISAIAH 54:17

Life Purpose

Dear God,
I know that you made me for a purpose,
and I need your help, please, Lord, to know what my
purpose is. Please clearly guide me in the best direction, so that
I can bring blessings and fulfillment through my work.

*The Lord will work out his plans for my life—
for your faithful love, O Lord, endures forever.*

PSALM 138:8

Marital Issues

Dear God,
My heart has been so open to loving
my spouse, but now it hurts and is numb.
Will you soften my heart and the heart of my partner, please,
so that we can regain our loving bond? Dear Lord, help us
communicate respectfully with one
another, even if we disagree.

First get rid of the log in your own eye;
then you will see well enough to deal with
the speck in your friend's eye.

MATTHEW 7:5

Moving

Dear God,
I sense that you are reassigning me to a new location,
and that you are guiding me to the right home, which is safe,
comfortable, and affordable. Please watch over me, Lord,
during this life transition, and give me peace
as I navigate these changes.

A house is built by wisdom and becomes strong through
good sense. Through knowledge its rooms are filled
with all sorts of precious riches and valuables.

PROVERBS 24:3–4

Partnership

Dear God,
I ask that you, who know the hearts
of everyone in the world, guide me to a healthy partnership
based upon mutual respect. Help me, Lord, to appreciate
and nurture my partnership, and soften both our
hearts with forgiveness and compassion.

*Be patient with each other, making allowance for each other's
faults because of your love. Make every effort to keep yourselves
united in the Spirit, binding yourselves together with peace.*

EPHESIANS 4:2–3

Pets

Dear God,
Thank you for creating animals; you know how much
I love [name of pet]. Can you please help [name of pet] with
[describe situation]? Please guide me in the best way
to help, and relieve me of worry, dear Lord.

The godly care for their animals.

PROVERBS 12:10

Protection, Emotional

Dear God,
I feel vulnerable and sensitive, and I don't know
if I can take any more emotional pain. Please, Lord, guard
my heart. Help me be wise in my choices of relationships
so that I can determine with whom to spend time, and
have the courage to let go of relationships that are
detracting from my relationship with you, Lord.

*Guard your heart above all else, for it determines
the course of your life.*

PROVERBS 4:23

Protection, Physical

Dear God,
Your strength and power are unparalleled,
and your protection is unstoppable. Please protect me, Lord,
and cast away anything that could harm me.
I am afraid, Lord, and need your protective love.

*Be strong in the Lord and in his mighty power. Put on all
of God's armor so that you will be able to stand firm
against all strategies of the devil.*

EPHESIANS 6:10–11

Protection, Spiritual

Dear God,
Please protect me from the tricks and temptations
of evil. Help me discern what is of you and what is not.
Dear Lord, who can see everything and who shines divine light
to cast away all darkness, give me the strength to say no
and walk away from that which is ungodly.

*So then let us cast off the works of darkness
and put on the armor of light.*

ROMANS 13:12 (ESV)

Reducing Fear

Dear God,
I admit that I feel nervous, insecure, vulnerable, and afraid.
Please bolster my courage, and help me be strong and brave.
I will rest in full faith and trust in your mighty power, God.

*Don't be afraid, for I am with you.
Don't be discouraged, for I am your God.
I will strengthen you and help you.
I will hold you up with my victorious right hand.*

ISAIAH 41:10

Self-Employment

Dear God,
You are my leader, my employer, my guidance counselor.
I am grateful for your Holy Spirit guiding and motivating
my career. I know that I'm not *self*-employed; I'm
God-employed, and therefore have nothing to fear.

*Work willingly at whatever you do, as though you were working
for the Lord rather than for people.*

COLOSSIANS 3:23

Simplifying Your Life

Dear God,
You are so powerful and awe-inspiring, and I believe that you
can see to the heart of everything and everyone. Please help me
release anything that is holding me back or pulling me down,
and focus only upon that which is a true priority.

*Then [Jesus] said, "Beware! Guard against every kind of greed.
Life is not measured by how much you own."*

LUKE 12:15

Sobriety

Dear God,
I desire to treat my body as a temple of Christ,
and I no longer want to pollute it with toxins.
Please, Lord, I need your help to be released from
the enslavement of my appetites, cravings, and insecurities.
Please remind me to prayerfully turn to you when
I'm feeling stressed, instead of to intoxicants.

For I can do everything through Christ, who gives me strength.

PHILIPPIANS **4:13**

Time Management

Dear God,
I have so many plans and ideas, and I ask that you help me sort
through them to know which are of you, and which are mis-
guided. Please help me zero in on my target priorities and have
the self-control to apportion time each day to work on them.

Live wisely among those who are not believers,
and make the most of every opportunity.

COLOSSIANS **4:5**

BIBLIOGRAPHY

GENERAL

"The Book of Tobit." *Holy Bible: King James Version*. EBible.org. http://ebible.org /kjv/Tobit.htm.

Holy Bible: English Standard Version. Wheaton, IL: Crossway Bibles, 2001.

Holy Bible: King James Version. BibleGateway.com. http://www.biblegateway.com /versions/King-James-Version-KJV-Bible

Holy Bible: New Living Translation. Carol Stream, IL: Tyndale House Publishers, 2015.

Laurence, Richard (translator). *The Book of Enoch the Prophet*. Kempton, IL: Adventures Unlimited Press, 2000.

PART I: THE HOLY TRINITY

"The Blessed Trinity." Catholic Online. http://www.catholic.org/encyclopedia /view.php?id=11699.

The Editors of Encyclopædia Britannica. "Trinity." Encyclopædia Britannica. September 15, 2017. https://www.britannica.com/topic/Trinity-Christianity.

Joyce, George. "The Blessed Trinity." *The Catholic Encyclopedia*. Vol. 15. New York: Robert Appleton Company, 1912. Retrieved from New Advent: http://www.newadvent.org/cathen/15047a.htm.

Lewis, C. S. *Mere Christianity: A Revised and Amplified Edition, with a New Introduction, of the Three Books, Broadcast Talks, Christian Behaviour, and Beyond Personality*. New York: HarperOne, 2009.

PART II: THE ANGELS

"Angels - Catholic Encyclopedia." Catholic Online. http://www.catholic.org /encyclopedia/view.php?id=774.

Aquinas, St. Thomas. *The Summa Theologiæ of St. Thomas Aquinas*. Literally translated by Fathers of the English Dominican Province. 2nd revised ed., 1920. Online 2016 edition copyright by Kevin Knight. Retrieved from New Advent: http://www.newadvent.org/summa/index.html.

Bunson, Matthew. *Angels A to Z: A Who's Who of the Heavenly Host*. New York: Three Rivers Press, 1996.

Charles, R. H. *The apocrypha and pseudepigrapha of the old Testament in English: with introductions and critical explanatory notes to the several books edited in conjunction with many scholars*. Oxford: Clarendon Press, 1913.

Corrigan, Kevin, and L. Michael Harrington. "Pseudo-Dionysius the Areopagite." Stanford Encyclopedia of Philosophy. September 06, 2004. https://plato.stanford.edu/entries/pseudo-dionysius-areopagite.

Driscoll, James F. "St. Raphael." *The Catholic Encyclopedia*. Vol. 12. New York: Robert Appleton Company, 1911. Retrieved from New Advent: http://www.newadvent.org/cathen/12640b.htm.

Holweck, Frederick. "St. Michael the Archangel." *The Catholic Encyclopedia*. Vol. 10. New York: Robert Appleton Company, 1911. Retrieved from New Advent: http://www.newadvent.org/cathen/10275b.htm

Lamarre, Mark. "Pseudo-Dionysius the Areopagite (fl. c. 650–c. 725 C.E.)." Internet Encyclopedia of Philosophy. http://www.iep.utm.edu/pseudodi.

Lewis, James R., and Evelyn Dorothy Oliver. *Angels A to Z*. Detroit, MI: Visible Ink Press, 1996.

"Michael, Gabriel and Raphael: Archangels and Powerful Allies - News." Catholic Online. http://www.catholic.org/news/national/story.php?id=34517.

Pope, Hugh. "Angels." *The Catholic Encyclopedia*. Vol. 1. New York: Robert Appleton Company, 1907. Retrieved from New Advent: http://www.newadvent.org/cathen/01476d.htm

Pope, Hugh. "St. Gabriel the Archangel." *The Catholic Encyclopedia*. Vol. 6. New York: Robert Appleton Company, 1909. Retrieved from New Advent: http://www.newadvent.org/cathen/06330a.htm

"St. Gabriel, the Archangel - Saints & Angels." Catholic Online. http://www.catholic.org/saints/saint.php?saint_id=279.

"St. Michael, the Archangel - Saints & Angels." Catholic Online. http://www.catholic.org/saints/saint.php?saint_id=308.

"St. Raphael - Saints & Angels." Catholic Online. http://www.catholic.org/saints/saint.php?saint_id=203.

"St. Uriel the Archangel." The Church of St. Uriel the Archangel. http://www.urielsg.org/our-patron-saint.

Wood, Alice. *Of Wings and Wheels: A Synthetic Study of the Biblical Cherubim*. Berlin: Walter de Gruyter, 2008.

PART III: THE SAINTS

"Adoration - Catholic Encyclopedia." Catholic Online. http://www.catholic.org/encyclopedia/view.php?id=228.

Catholic Answers. "Praying to the Saints." San Diego, CA: Catholic Answers, 2004. https://www.catholic.com/tract/praying-to-the-saints.

Craughwell, Thomas J. *Saints for Every Occasion: 101 of Heaven's Most Powerful Patrons*. Charlotte, NC: Stampley Enterprises, Inc., 2001.

Jones, Kathleen. *Women Saints: Lives of Faith and Courage*. Kent, England: Burns & Oates, 1999.

La Plante, Alice and Clare. *Heaven Help Us: The Worrier's Guide to the Patron Saints*. New York: Dell Publishing, 1999.

Makarios, Hieromonk, of Simonos Petra. *The Synaxarion: The Lives of Saints of the Orthodox Church*. Vol. 1. Chalkidike, Greece: The Holy Convent of the Annunciation of Our Lady, Ormylia, 1998.

Paul, Tessa. *An Illustrated Dictionary of Saints: A Guide to the Lives and Works of Over 300 of the World's Most Notable Saints, with Expert Commentary and More Than 350 Beautiful Illustrations.* London: Anness Publishing Limited, 2017.

"Saint." Merriam-Webster. https://www.merriam-webster.com/dictionary/saint.

Trinity Communications. "Hyperdulia." CatholicCulture.org. https://www .catholicculture.org/culture/library/dictionary/index.cfm?id=34033.

ST. AGATHA

The Editors of Encyclopædia Britannica. "St. Agatha." Encyclopædia Britannica. March 10, 2017. https://www.britannica.com/biography/Saint-Agatha.

Kirsch, Johann Peter. "St. Agatha." *The Catholic Encyclopedia.* Vol. 1. New York: Robert Appleton Company, 1907. Retrieved from New Advent: http://www .newadvent.org/cathen/01203c.htm.

Marie, Brother André. "Saint Agatha's Breasts." Catholicism.org. February 5, 2014. http://catholicism.org/saint-agathas-breasts.html.

Miller, Fr. Don. "Saint Agatha: Saint of the Day for February 5." Franciscan Media. https://www.franciscanmedia.org/saint-agatha.

"St. Agatha - Saints & Angels." Catholic Online. http://www.catholic.org/saints /saint.php?saint_id=14.

ST. ANNE

The Editors of Encyclopædia Britannica. "Saints Anne and Joachim." Encyclopædia Britannica. November 28, 2012. https://www.britannica.com/biography/Saint -Anne.

Holweck, Frederick. "St. Anne." *The Catholic Encyclopedia.* Vol. 1. New York: Robert Appleton Company, 1907. Retrieved from New Advent: http://www.new advent.org/cathen/01538a.htm.

"Saint Anne." CatholicSaints.Info. August 30, 2017. https://catholicsaints.info /saint-anne.

"Sts. Joachim and Anne - Saints & Angels." Catholic Online. http://www.catholic .org/saints/saint.php?saint_id=22.

ST. ANTHONY

Dal-Gal, Niccolò. "St. Anthony of Padua." *The Catholic Encyclopedia.* Vol. 1. New York: Robert Appleton Company, 1907. Retrieved from New Advent: http://www .newadvent.org/cathen/01556a.htm.

The Editors of Encyclopædia Britannica. "St. Anthony of Padua." Encyclopædia Britannica. June 20, 2017. https://www.britannica.com/biography/Saint-Anthony -of-Padua.

"St. Anthony of Padua - Saints & Angels." Catholic Online. http://www.catholic .org/saints/saint.php?saint_id=24.

ST. BARBARA

The Editors of Encyclopædia Britannica. "St. Barbara." Encyclopædia Britannica. March 24, 2017. https://www.britannica.com/biography/Saint-Barbara.

"Greatmartyr Barbara at Heliopolis, in Syria." Orthodox Church in America. https://oca.org/saints/lives/2017/12/04/103472-greatmartyr-barbara-at-heliopolis -in-syria.

Kirsch, Johann Peter. "St. Barbara." *The Catholic Encyclopedia*. Vol. 2. New York: Robert Appleton Company, 1907. Retrieved from New Advent: http://www .newadvent.org/cathen/02284d.htm.

"St. Barbara - Saints & Angels." Catholic Online. http://www.catholic.org/saints /saint.php?saint_id=166.

St. Benedict

Ford, Hugh. "St. Benedict of Nursia." *The Catholic Encyclopedia*. Vol. 2. New York: Robert Appleton Company, 1907. Retrieved from New Advent: http://www .newadvent.org/cathen/02467b.htm.

Knowles, Michael David. "Saint Benedict." Encyclopædia Britannica. September 26, 2016. https://www.britannica.com/biography/Saint-Benedict-of-Nursia.

Miller, Fr. Don. "Saint Benedict." Franciscan Media. https://www.franciscanmedia .org/saint-benedict.

"St. Benedict of Nursia - Saints & Angels." Catholic Online. http://www.catholic .org/saints/saint.php?saint_id=556.

"St. Benedict - Saints & Angels." Catholic Online. http://www.catholic.org/saints /saint.php?saint_id=26.

St. Bernadette of Lourdes

Bertrin, Georges. "Notre-Dame de Lourdes." *The Catholic Encyclopedia*. Vol. 9. New York: Robert Appleton Company, 1910. Retrieved from New Advent: http://www .newadvent.org/cathen/09389b.htm.

The Editors of Encyclopædia Britannica. "St. Bernadette of Lourdes." Encyclopædia Britannica. March 24, 2017. https://www.britannica.com/biography/Saint -Bernadette-of-Lourdes.

Foley, Anthony. "St Bernadette: 'My business is to be ill.'" *The Catholic Herald* (UK). December 10, 2008. Retrieved from Catholic Online: http://www.catholic .org/news/international/europe/story.php?id=30965.

"St. Bernadette - Saints & Angels." Catholic Online. http://www.catholic.org /saints/saint.php?saint_id=147.

"St. Bernadette Soubirous - Saints & Angels." Catholic Online. http://www .catholic.org/saints/saint.php?saint_id=1757.

St. Catherine of Alexandria

Clugnet, Léon. "St. Catherine of Alexandria." *The Catholic Encyclopedia*. Vol. 3. New York: Robert Appleton Company, 1908. Retrieved from New Advent: http:// www.newadvent.org/cathen/03445a.htm.

The Editors of Encyclopædia Britannica. "St. Catherine of Alexandria." Encyclopædia Britannica. March 28, 2017. https://www.britannica.com/biography /Saint-Catherine-of-Alexandria.

"St. Catherine of Alexandria – Catholic Encyclopedia." Catholic Online. http:// www.catholic.org/encyclopedia/view.php?id=2673.

"St. Catherine of Alexandria - Saints & Angels." Catholic Online. http://www
.catholic.org/saints/saint.php?saint_id=341.

St. Catherine of Siena

The Editors of Encyclopædia Britannica. "St. Catherine of Siena." Encyclopædia
Britannica. https://www.britannica.com/biography/Saint-Catherine-of-Siena.

Gardner, Edmund. "St. Catherine of Siena." *The Catholic Encyclopedia*. Vol. 3. New
York: Robert Appleton Company, 1908. Retrieved from New Advent: http://www
.newadvent.org/cathen/03447a.htm.

"St. Catherine of Siena: Doctor of the Church – Christian Saints & Heroes."
Catholic Online. http://www.catholic.org/news/saints/story.php?id=41236.

 "St. Catherine of Siena - Saints & Angels." Catholic Online. http://www.catholic
.org/saints/saint.php?saint_id=9.

St. Cecilia

The Editors of Encyclopædia Britannica. "St. Cecilia." Encyclopædia Britannica.
March 24, 2017. https://www.britannica.com/biography/Saint-Cecilia.

Kirsch, Johann Peter. "St. Cecilia." *The Catholic Encyclopedia*. Vol. 3. New York:
Robert Appleton Company, 1908. Retrieved from New Advent: http://www
.newadvent.org/cathen/03471b.htm.

"St. Cecilia - Catholic Encyclopedia." Catholic Online. http://www.catholic.org
/encyclopedia/view.php?id=2709.

"St. Cecilia - Saints & Angels." Catholic Online. http://www.catholic.org/saints
/saint.php?saint_id=34.

St. Christopher

The Editors of Encyclopædia Britannica. "Saint Christopher." Encyclopædia Britannica. January 12, 2014. https://www.britannica.com/biography/Saint
-Christopher.

Mershman, Francis. "St. Christopher." *The Catholic Encyclopedia*. Vol. 3. New
York: Robert Appleton Company, 1908. Retrieved from New Advent: http://
www.newadvent.org/cathen/03728a.htm.

"St. Christopher - Catholic Encyclopedia." Catholic Online. http://www.catholic
.org/encyclopedia/view.php?id=2935.

"St. Christopher - Saints & Angels." Catholic Online. http://www.catholic.org
/saints/saint.php?saint_id=36.

St. Clare of Assisi

The Editors of Encyclopædia Britannica. "St. Clare of Assisi." Encyclopædia
Britannica. March 17, 2017. https://www.britannica.com/biography/Saint-Clare
-of-Assisi.

Robinson, Paschal. "St. Clare of Assisi." *The Catholic Encyclopedia*. Vol. 4. New
York: Robert Appleton Company, 1908. Retrieved from New Advent: http://www
.newadvent.org/cathen/04004a.htm.

"St. Clare of Assisi - Catholic Encyclopedia." Catholic Online. http://www
.catholic.org/encyclopedia/view.php?id=2999.

"St. Clare of Assisi - Saints & Angels." Catholic Online. http://www.catholic.org /saints/saint.php?saint_id=215.

ST. DYMPHNA

Kirsch, Johann Peter. "St. Dymphna." *The Catholic Encyclopedia*. Vol. 5. New York: Robert Appleton Company, 1909. Retrieved from New Advent: http:// www.newadvent.org/cathen/05221b.htm.

"Saint Dymphna." CatholicSaints.Info. August 4, 2017. https://catholicsaints .info/saint-dymphna.

"St. Dymphna - Catholic Encyclopedia." Catholic Online. http://www.catholic .org/encyclopedia/view.php?id=4107.

"St. Dymphna - Saints & Angels." Catholic Online. http://www.catholic.org /saints/saint.php?saint_id=222.

ST. FAUSTINA KOWALSKA

Kowalska, Maria Faustina. *Diary of Saint Maria Faustina Kowalska: Divine Mercy in My Soul*. Stockbridge, MA: Marian Press, 2005. Retrieved from Archive.org: https:// archive.org/details/St.FaustinaKowalskaDiary.

"Mary Faustina Kowalska." Vatican: the Holy See. http://www.vatican.va /news_services/liturgy/documents/ns_lit_doc_20000430_faustina_en.html.

"Saint Faustina Kowalska." CatholicSaints.Info. October 5, 2017. https:// catholicsaints.info/saint-faustina-kowalska.

"St. Faustina Kowalska - Saints & Angels." Catholic Online. http://www.catholic .org/saints/saint.php?saint_id=510.

ST. FLORIAN

Magnifico, Laura. "St. Florian: How He Became Patron Saint of Firefighters." Catholic Faith Store. https://blog.catholicfaithstore.com/st-florian-how-he -became-patron-saint-of-firefighters.

"Saint Florian." Saint Florian Roman Catholic Church. http://www.stflorian parish.org/history/saint-florian.

"Saint Florian of Lorch." CatholicSaints.Info. May 7, 2017. https://catholicsaints .info/saint-florian-of-lorch.

"St. Florian - Saints & Angels." Catholic Online. http://www.catholic.org/saints /saint.php?saint_id=149.

ST. FRANCIS OF ASSISI

Catholic Online. "St. Francis of Assisi - Saints & Angels - Catholic Online." Catholic Online. http://www.catholic.org/saints/saint.php?saint_id=50.

Miles, Margaret R. *The Word Made Flesh: A History of Christian Thought*. Oxford: Wiley-Blackwell, 2006.

Miller, Fr. Don. "Saint Francis of Assisi: Saint of the Day for October 4." Franciscan Media. https://www.franciscanmedia.org/saint-francis-of-assisi.

St. Gemma Galgani

Bell, Rudolph M., and Cristina Mazzoni. *The Voices of Gemma Galgani: The Life and Afterlife of a Modern Saint.* Chicago: University of Chicago Press, 2003.

Dallaire, Glen. St Gemma Galgani. http://www.stgemmagalgani.com.

"Saint Gemma Galgani," CatholicSaints.Info. July 9, 2017. https://catholicsaints .info/saint-gemma-galgani.

"St. Gemma Galgani - Saints & Angels." Catholic Online. http://www.catholic .org/saints/saint.php?saint_id=225.

St. Gerard

The Editors of Encyclopædia Britannica. "St. Gerard." Encyclopædia Britannica. February 6, 2017. https://www.britannica.com/biography/Saint-Gerard.

Magnier, John. "St. Gerard Majella." *The Catholic Encyclopedia.* Vol. 6. New York: Robert Appleton Company, 1909. Retrieved from New Advent: http://www .newadvent.org/cathen/06467c.htm.

"Saints: St. Gerard Majella." The Redemptorists of Australia and New Zealand. http://cssr.com/english/saintsblessed/stmajella.shtml.

"St. Gerard Majella: Celebrant of Life." The Redemptorists of Australia and New Zealand. https://www.cssr.org.au/about_us/default.cfm?loadref=65.

"St. Gerard Majella - Saints & Angels." Catholic Online. http://www.catholic.org /saints/saint.php?saint_id=150.

St. Hildegard of Bingen

The Editors of Encyclopædia Britannica. "St. Hildegarde." Encyclopædia Britannica. June 18, 2014. https://www.britannica.com/biography/Saint-Hildegard.

Hildegard of Bingen. *Hildegard of Bingen: Selected Writings.* Translated by Mark Atherton. New York: Penguin, 2001.

International Society of Hildegard von Bingen Studies. http://www.hildegard -society.org.

Mershman, Francis. "St. Hildegard." *The Catholic Encyclopedia.* Vol. 7. New York: Robert Appleton Company, 1910. Retrieved from New Advent: http:// www.newadvent.org/cathen/07351a.htm.

"The Patron Saints of the Culinary Arts. Loyola Press." https://www.loyolapress .com/our-catholic-faith/prayer/arts-and-faith/culinary-arts/the-patron-saints-of -the-culinary-arts.

"St. Hildegarde - Catholic Encyclopedia." Catholic Online. http://www.catholic .org/encyclopedia/view.php?id=5777.

"St. Hildegarde - Saints & Angels." Catholic Online. http://www.catholic.org /saints/saint.php?saint_id=285.

St. Joan of Arc

Bie, Søren. Jeanne d'Arc la Pucelle. https://www.jeanne-darc.info.

Lanhers, Yvonne, and Malcolm G.A. Vale. "Saint Joan of Arc." Encyclopædia Britannica. https://www.britannica.com/biography/Saint-Joan-of-Arc.

"Saint Joan of Arc." CatholicSaints.Info. October 7, 2017. https://catholicsaints
.info/saint-joan-of-arc.

"St. Joan of Arc - Catholic Encyclopedia." Catholic Online. http://www.catholic
.org/encyclopedia/view.php?id=6346.

"St. Joan of Arc - Saints & Angels." Catholic Online. http://www.catholic.org
/saints/saint.php?saint_id=295.

Thurston, Herbert. "St. Joan of Arc." *The Catholic Encyclopedia*. Vol. 8. New
York: Robert Appleton Company, 1910. Retrieved from New Advent: http://
www.newadvent.org/cathen/ 08409c.htm.

St. John of the Cross

The Editors of Encyclopædia Britannica. "St. John of the Cross." Encyclopædia
Britannica. June 18, 2015. https://www.britannica.com/biography//Saint-John-of
-the-Cross.

Saint John of the Cross. *Dark Night of the Soul: And Other Great Works*. Edited by
Lloyd B. Hildebrand. Orlando, FL: Bridge-Logos, 2007.

"St. John of the Cross - Catholic Encyclopedia." Catholic Online. http://www
.catholic.org/encyclopedia/view.php?id=6432.

"St. John of the Cross - Saints & Angels." Catholic Online. http://www.catholic
.org/saints/saint.php?saint_id=65.

Zimmerman, Benedict. "St. John of the Cross." *The Catholic Encyclopedia*. Vol. 8.
New York: Robert Appleton Company, 1910. Retrieved from New Advent: http://
www.newadvent.org/cathen/08480a.htm.

St. John the Baptist

Souvay, Charles. "St. John the Baptist." *The Catholic Encyclopedia*. Vol. 8. New
York: Robert Appleton Company, 1910. Retrieved from New Advent: http://www
.newadvent.org/cathen/08486b.htm.

"St. John the Baptist - Catholic Encyclopedia." Catholic Online. http://www
.catholic.org/encyclopedia/view.php?id=6448.

"St. John the Baptist - Saints & Angels." Catholic Online. http://www.catholic
.org/saints/saint.php?saint_id=152.

Strugnell, John. "St. John the Baptist." Encyclopædia Britannica. https://www
.britannica.com/biography/Saint-John-the-Baptist.

St. Joseph

The Editors of Encyclopædia Britannica. "St. Joseph." Encyclopædia Britannica.
May 25, 2017. https://www.britannica.com/biography/Saint-Joseph.

"Saint Joseph." CatholicSaints.Info. October 15, 2017. https://catholicsaints.info
/saint-joseph.

Souvay, Charles. "St. Joseph." *The Catholic Encyclopedia*. Vol. 8. New York:
Robert Appleton Company, 1910. Retrieved from New Advent: http://www
.newadvent.org/cathen/08504a.htm.

"St. Joseph - Saints & Angels." Catholic Online. http://www.catholic.org/saints
/saint.php?saint_id=4.

St. Jude

Camerlynck, Achille. "Epistle of St. Jude." *The Catholic Encyclopedia*. Vol. 8. New York: Robert Appleton Company, 1910. Retrieved from New Advent: http://www.newadvent.org/cathen/08542b.htm.

The National Shrine of St. Jude. http://www.shrineofstjude.org.

New World Encyclopedia contributors. "Jude the Apostle." New World Encyclopedia. May 24, 2014. http://www.newworldencyclopedia.org/p/index.php?title=Jude_the_Apostle&oldid=981780.

"Saint Jude Thaddeus." CatholicSaints.Info. October 4, 2017. https://catholicsaints.info/saint-jude-thaddeus.

"St. Jude Thaddaeus - Saints & Angels." Catholic Online. http://www.catholic.org/saints/saint.php?saint_id=127.

St. Kateri Tekakwitha

"Blessed Kateri Tekakwitha - Catholic Encyclopedia." Catholic Online. http://www.catholic.org/encyclopedia/view.php?id=6594.

The Editors of Encyclopædia Britannica. "St. Kateri Tekakwitha." Encyclopædia Britannica. July 31, 2017. https://www.britannica.com/biography/Saint-Kateri-Tekakwitha.

Kelly, Blanche Mary. "Blessed Kateri Tekakwitha." *The Catholic Encyclopedia*. Vol. 14. New York: Robert Appleton Company, 1912. Retrieved from New Advent: http://www.newadvent.org/cathen/14471a.htm.

Mary, Brother Joseph, MICM. "Saint Kateri Tekakwitha." Catholicism.org. July 11, 2005. http://catholicism.org/kateri-tekakwitha.html.

"St. Kateri Tekakwitha - Saints & Angels." Catholic Online. http://www.catholic.org/saints/saint.php?saint_id=154.

St. Maria Goretti

Buehrle, Marie Cecilia. *Saint Maria Goretti*. Milwaukee, WI: Bruce Publishing Company, 1950.

Miller, Fr. Don. "Saint Maria Goretti." Franciscan Media. https://www.franciscanmedia.org/saint-maria-goretti.

"Saint Maria Goretti." CatholicSaints.Info. October 8, 2017. https://catholicsaints.info/saint-maria-goretti.

"St. Maria Goretti - Saints & Angels." Catholic Online. http://www.catholic.org/saints/saint.php?saint_id=78.

Treasures of the Church. *St. Maria Goretti: The Little Saint of Great Mercy*. http://mariagoretti.com.

St. Mary Magdalene

Ehrman, Bart D. *Peter, Paul, and Mary Magdalene: The Followers of Jesus in History and Legend*. 2nd ed. Oxford: Oxford University Press, 2006.

Lyons, Eric. "The Real Mary Magdalene." Apologetics Press. 2006. http://www.apologeticspress.org/APContent.aspx?category=10&article=1803.

New World Encyclopedia contributers. "Mary Magadalene." New World Encyclopedia. August 28, 2014. http://www.newworldencyclopedia.org /entry/Mary_Magdalene.

Paul, Pope John, II. "Apostolic Letter Mulieris Dignitatem of the Supreme Pontiff John Paul II on the Dignity and Vocation of Women on the Occasion of the Marian Year." Vatican: The Holy See. August 15, 1988. https://w2.vatican.va/content /john-paul-ii/en/apost_letters/1988/documents/hf_jp-ii_apl_19880815_mulieris -dignitatem.html

Pope, Hugh. "St. Mary Magdalen." *The Catholic Encyclopedia*. Vol. 9. New York: Robert Appleton Company, 1910. Retrieved from New Advent: http://www .newadvent.org/cathen/09761a.htm.

Thompson, Mary R. *Mary of Magdala: Apostle and Leader*. 2nd ed. New York: Paulist Press, 1995.

ST. MARY THE BLESSED VIRGIN

The Editors of Encyclopædia Britannica. "Mary Mother of Jesus." Encyclopædia Britannica. October 12, 2017. https://www.britannica.com/biography/Mary -mother-of-Jesus.

Flinn, Frank K. *Encyclopedia of Catholicism (Encyclopedia of World Religions)*. New York: Facts on File, 2007.

Maas, Anthony. "The Blessed Virgin Mary." *The Catholic Encyclopedia*. Vol. 15. New York: Robert Appleton Company, 1912. Retrieved from New Advent: http:// www.newadvent.org/cathen/15464b.htm.

McNally, Terry. *What Every Catholic Should Know About Mary: Dogmas, Doctrines, and Devotions*. Bloomington, IN: Xlibris Corp., 2009.

Trinity Communications. "Hyperdulia." CatholicCulture.org. https://www .catholicculture.org/culture/library/dictionary/index.cfm?id=34033.

ST. MAXIMILIAN KOLBE

Armstrong, Regis J, and Ingrid J Peterson. *The Franciscan Tradition: Franciscan Tradition (Spirituality in History)*. Collegeville, MN: Liturgical Press, 2010.

Catholic Online. "St. Maximilian Kolbe - Saints & Angels - Catholic Online." Catholic Online. http://www.catholic.org/saints/saint.php?saint_id=370.

Michael, Robert. *A History of Catholic Antisemitism: The Dark Side of the Church*. Basingstoke, England: Palgrave Macmillan, 2008.

Treece, Patricia. *A Man for Others: Maximilian Kolbe, Saint of Auschwitz, in the Words of Those Who Knew Him*. New York: Harper & Row, 1982.

ST. MOTHER TERESA

Mukherjee, Bharati. "Mother Teresa: The Saint." *Time Magazine*. June 14, 1999. http://content.time.com/time/magazine/article/0,9171,991258,00.html.

"Mother Teresa - Biographical." Nobelprize.org. Nobel Media AB. 2014. http:// www.nobelprize.org/nobel_prizes/peace/laureates/1979/teresa-bio.html.

Mother Teresa et al. *No Greater Love*. 1st ed. Novato, CA: New World Library, 2002.

"Mother Teresa of Calcutta (1910–1997), Biography." Vatican: the Holy See. http://www.vatican.va/news_services/liturgy/saints/ns_lit_doc_20031019_madre -teresa_en.html.

St. Nicholas

Federer, William J. "There Really Is a Santa Claus - History of Saint Nicholas & Christmas Holiday Tradition." St. Louis, MO: Amerisearch, Inc., 2003.

Ott, Michael. "St. Nicholas of Myra." *The Catholic Encyclopedia*. Vol. 11. New York: Robert Appleton Company, 1911. Retrieved from New Advent: http://www.newadvent.org/cathen/11063b.htm.

"Saint Nicholas of Myra." CatholicSaints.Info. October 5, 2017. https://catholicsaints.info/saint-nicholas-of-myra.

"St. Nicholas Center: Who Is St. Nicholas?" St. Nicholas Center: Discovering the Truth About Santa Claus. http://www.stnicholascenter.org/pages/who-is-st-nicholas.

St. Padre Pio

Bertanzetti, Eileen Dunn, ed. *Padre Pio's Words of Hope*. Huntington, IN: Our Sunday Visitor, 1999.

Corsi, Jerome R. *The Shroud Codex*. New York: Threshold Editions, 2010.

Ruffin, Bernard. *Padre Pio*. 3rd ed. Huntington, IN: Our Sunday Visitor, 1991.

"Saint Padre Pio." CatholicSaints.Info. October 8, 2017. https://catholicsaints.info/saint-padre-pio.

St. Patrick

Bos, Carole "St. Patrick's Cross" AwesomeStories.com. https://www.awesomestories.com/asset/view/St.-Patrick-s-Cross.

Grattan-Flood, William. "St. Patrick's Purgatory." *The Catholic Encyclopedia*. Vol. 12. New York: Robert Appleton Company, 1911. Retrieved from New Advent: http://www.newadvent.org/cathen/12580a.htm.

Moran, Patrick Francis Cardinal. "St. Patrick." *The Catholic Encyclopedia*. Vol. 11. New York: Robert Appleton Company, 1911. Retrieved from New Advent: http://www.newadvent.org/cathen/11554a.htm.

"Saint Patrick." CatholicSaints.Info. November 29, 2017. https://catholicsaints.info/saint-patrick.

St. Patrick. *The Confession of St. Patrick*. Retrieved from Christian Classics Ethereal Library: http://www.ccel.org/ccel/patrick/confession.html.

St. Paul

Ehrman, Bart D. *Peter, Paul, and Mary Magdalene: The Followers of Jesus in History and Legend*. 2nd ed. Oxford: Oxford University Press, 2006.

Maccoby, Hyam. *The Mythmaker: Paul and the Invention of Christianity*. New York: Barnes & Noble, 1998.

Prat, Ferdinand. "St. Paul." *The Catholic Encyclopedia*. Vol. 11. New York: Robert Appleton Company, 1911. Retrieved from New Advent: http://www.newadvent.org/cathen/11567b.htm.

"Saint Paul the Apostle." CatholicSaints.Info. October 6, 2017. https://catholicsaints.info/saint-paul-the-apostle.

St. Peter

Ehrman, Bart D. "Peter, Paul, and Mary Magdalene: The Followers of Jesus in History and Legend." 2nd ed.,Oxford, Oxford University Press, 2006.

Kirsch, Johann Peter. "St. Peter, Prince of the Apostles." *The Catholic Encyclopedia*. Vol. 11. New York: Robert Appleton Company, 1911. Retrieved from New Advent: http://www.newadvent.org/cathen/11744a.htm.

"Saint Peter the Apostle." CatholicSaints.Info. October 6, 2017. https://catholic saints.info/saint-peter-the-apostle.

St. Philomena

Catholic Online. "St. Philomena - Saints & Angels - Catholic Online." Catholic Online. http://www.catholic.org/saints/saint.php?saint_id=98.

Kirsch, Johann Peter. "St. Philomena." *The Catholic Encyclopedia*. Vol. 12. New York: Robert Appleton Company, 1911. Retrieved from New Advent: http://www .newadvent.org/cathen/12025b.htm.

"Saint Philomena." CatholicSaints.Info. August 11, 2017. https://catholicsaints .info/saint-philomena.

"St. Philomena: Patron Saint Of Babies, Infants, and Youth." Stphilomenaparish .com. http://www.stphilomenaparish.com/patron.htm.

St. Rita of Cascia

Freze, Michael. *They Bore the Wounds of Christ: The Mystery of the Sacred Stigmata*. Huntington, IN: Our Sunday Visitor Publishing, 1989.

Mershman, Francis. "St. Rita of Cascia." *The Catholic Encyclopedia*. Vol. 13. New York: Robert Appleton Company, 1912. Retrieved from New Advent: http://www .newadvent.org/cathen/13064a.htm.

"Saint Rita of Cascia." CatholicSaints.Info. August 4, 2017. https://catholicsaints .info/saint-rita-of-cascia.

"The Story of St. Rita of Cascia | Saint Rita Catholic Church." Saint Rita Catholic Church. 2017. https://st-rita.org/the-story-of-st-rita-of-cascia.

St. Sebastian

Löffler, Klemens. "St. Sebastian." *The Catholic Encyclopedia*. Vol. 13. New York: Robert Appleton Company, 1912. Retrieved from New Advent: http://www .newadvent.org/cathen/13668a.htm.

"Saint Sebastian." CatholicSaints.Info. July 16, 2017. https://catholicsaints.info /saint-sebastian.

Zupnick, Irving L. "Saint Sebastian: The Vicissitudes of the Hero as Martyr." *Concepts of the Hero in the Middle Ages and the Renaissance*. Albany, NY: State University of New York Press, 1975.

St. Teresa of Ávila

Carroll Cruz, Joan. *The Incorruptibles: A Study of the Incorruption of the Bodies of Various Catholic Saints and Beati*. 3rd ed. Rockford, IL: TAN Books, 1991.

Slade, Carole. *St. Teresa of Avila: Author of a Heroic Life*. Berkeley, CA: University of California Press, 1995.

Walsh, William Thomas. *Saint Teresa of Avila*. Charlotte, NC: TAN Books, 2009.

St. Thérèse of Lisieux

The Editors of Encyclopædia Britannica. "Saint Thérèse of Lisieux." Encyclopædia Britannica. April 1, 2017. https://www.britannica.com/biography/Saint-Therese -of-Lisieux.

Conn, Joann Wolski. "Thérèse of Lisieux." *Christian Spirituality: The Classics*. New York: Routledge, 2009.

de Lisieux, St. Thérèse. *Story of a Soul: The Autobiography of St. Therese of Lisieux (the Little Flower)*. 3rd ed. Translated by John Clarke. Washington, D.C.: ICS Publications, 1996.

Donovan, Edith. "St. Thérèse of Lisieux." *The Catholic Encyclopedia*. Vol. 17 (Supplement). New York: The Encyclopedia Press, 1922. Retrieved from New Advent: http://www.newadvent.org/cathen/17721a.htm.

Payne, Steven. *Saint Thérèse of Lisieux: Doctor of the Universal Church*. Staten Island, NY: Saint Pauls/Alba House, 2002.

Schwarz, Josef. "Therese von Lisieux." *Renascence* 5, no. 1 (1952): 47–48. doi:10.5840/renascence19525140.

St. Thomas Aquinas

Chenu, Marie-Dominique. "St. Thomas Aquinas." Encyclopædia Britannica. June 20, 2017. https://www.britannica.com/biography/Saint-Thomas-Aquinas.

Gilson, Etienne. *The Christian Philosophy of St. Thomas Aquinas*. Notre Dame, IN: University of Notre Dame Press, 1994.

Kennedy, Daniel. "St. Thomas Aquinas." *The Catholic Encyclopedia*. Vol. 14. New York: Robert Appleton Company, 1912. Retrieved from New Advent: http://www .newadvent.org/cathen/14663b.htm.

King, Peter. "St. Thomas Aquinas." *International Philosophical Quarterly* 23, no. 2 (1983): 227–229.

McInerny, Ralph. *St. Thomas Aquinas*. Notre Dame, IN: University of Notre Dame Press, 1982.

St. Thomas More

Donnelly, Sister Gertrude. "St. Thomas More." *The Catholic Lawyer* 14, no. 4 (2016): 7.

Gilman, Richard. "St. Thomas More." *The Catholic Lawyer* 1, no. 1 (2016): 6.

Huddleston, Gilbert. "St. Thomas More." *The Catholic Encyclopedia*. Vol. 14. New York: Robert Appleton Company, 1912. Retrieved from New Advent: http://www .newadvent.org/cathen/14689c.htm.

Mahoney, Mother M. Denis. "St. Thomas More." *The Catholic Historical Review* 41, no. 1 (April 1955): 50–52.

Marc'hadour, Germain P. "Thomas More." Encyclopædia Britannica. October 17, 2017. https://www.britannica.com/biography/Thomas-More-English-humanist -and-statesman.

ST. VALENTINE

The Editors of Encyclopædia Britannica. "Saint Valentine." Encyclopædia Britannica. February 17, 2017. https://www.britannica.com/biography/Saint-Valentine.

Kelly, Henry Ansgar. *Chaucer and the Cult of Saint Valentine*. Vol. 5. Leiden, The Netherlands: Brill, 1986.

Oruch, Jack B. "St. Valentine, Chaucer, and Spring in February." *Speculum* 56, no. 3 (1981): 534–565.

Schmidt, Leigh Eric. "The Fashioning of a Modern Holiday: St. Valentine's Day, 1840–1870." *Winterthur Portfolio* 28, no. 4 (1993): 209–245.

Thurston, Herbert. "St. Valentine." *The Catholic Encyclopedia*. Vol. 15. New York: Robert Appleton Company, 1912. Retrieved from New Advent: http://www.newadvent.org/cathen/15254a.htm.

ABOUT THE AUTHOR

Doreen Virtue graduated from Chapman University with two degrees in counseling psychology. A former psychotherapist, Doreen now gives online workshops on topics related to her books and card decks. She's the author of *Mornings with the Lord*, *The Courage to Be Creative*, and the *Loving Words from Jesus Cards*, among many other works. She has appeared on *Oprah*, CNN, the BBC, *The View*, and *Good Morning America* and has been featured in newspapers and magazines worldwide.

Raised by her parents in New Thought religion, Doreen found that her spiritual path was forever changed by a vision of Jesus in January 2017, which led her to become baptized as a Christian. Her work now focuses on gently helping people reconnect with the real Jesus, as well as advocating for animal rights and supporting her favorite charity, Compassion International, which helps impoverished children worldwide.

For information on Doreen's work, please visit her at AngelTherapy.com or Facebook.com/DoreenVirtue444. To enroll in Doreen's video courses, please visit www.EarthAngel.com.

Hay House Titles of Related Interest

YOU CAN HEAL YOUR LIFE, the movie, starring Louise Hay & Friends
(available as a 1-DVD program, an expanded
2-DVD set, and streaming online video)
Learn more at www.hayhouse.com/louise-movie

THE SHIFT, the movie, starring Dr. Wayne W. Dyer
(available as a 1-DVD program an expanded
2-DVD set, and streaming online video)
Learn more at www.hayhouse.com/the-shift-movie

THE BOY WHO MET JESUS:
Segatashya Emmanuel of Kibeho, by Immaculée Ilibagiza

FOR LOVERS OF GOD EVERYWHERE:
Poems of the Christian Mystics, by Roger Housden

THE ROSARY: The Prayer that Saved My Life,
by Immaculée Ilibagiza

WRITING IN THE SAND: Jesus, Spirituality,
and the Soul of the Gospels, by Thomas Moore

All of the above are available at your local bookstore,
or may be ordered by contacting Hay House (see next page).

Free e-newsletters from Hay House, the Ultimate Resource for Inspiration

Be the first to know about Hay House's free downloads, special offers, giveaways, contests, and more!

 Get exclusive excerpts from our latest releases and videos from *Hay House Present Moments*.

 Our *Digital Products Newsletter* is the perfect way to stay up-to-date on our latest discounted eBooks, featured mobile apps, and Live Online and On Demand events.

 Learn with real benefits! *HayHouseU.com* is your source for the most innovative online courses from the world's leading personal growth experts. Be the first to know about new online courses and to receive exclusive discounts.

 Enjoy uplifting personal stories, how-to articles, and healing advice, along with videos and empowering quotes, within *Heal Your Life*.

 Have an inspirational story to tell and a passion for writing? Sharpen your writing skills with insider tips from *Your Writing Life*.

Sign Up Now!

Get inspired, educate yourself, get a complimentary gift, and share the wisdom!

Visit www.hayhouse.com/newsletters to sign up today!

 HAY HOUSE

 HAYHOUSE RADIO)) *radio for your soul®*

 HAYHOUSE online learning

Hay House Podcasts
Bring Fresh, Free Inspiration Each Week!

Hay House proudly offers a selection of life-changing audio content via our most popular podcasts!

Hay House Meditations Podcast

Features your favorite Hay House authors guiding you through meditations designed to help you relax and rejuvenate. Take their words into your soul and cruise through the week!

Dr. Wayne W. Dyer Podcast

Discover the timeless wisdom of Dr. Wayne W. Dyer, world-renowned spiritual teacher and affectionately known as "the father of motivation". Each week brings some of the best selections from the 10-year span of Dr. Dyer's talk show on HayHouseRadio.com.

Hay House World Summit Podcast

Over 1 million people from 217 countries and territories participate in the massive online event known as the Hay House World Summit. This podcast offers weekly mini-lessons from World Summits past as a taste of what you can hear during the annual event, which occurs each May.

Hay House Radio Podcast

Listen to some of the best moments from HayHouseRadio.com, featuring expert authors such as Dr. Christiane Northrup, Anthony William, Caroline Myss, James Van Praagh, and Doreen Virtue discussing topics such as health, self-healing, motivation, spirituality, positive psychology, and personal development.

Hay House Live Podcast

Enjoy a selection of insightful and inspiring lectures from Hay House Live, an exciting event series that features Hay House authors and leading experts in the fields of alternative health, nutrition, intuitive medicine, success, and more! Feel the electricity of our authors engaging with a live audience, and get motivated to live your best life possible!

Find Hay House podcasts on iTunes, or visit
www.HayHouse.com/podcasts for more info.